It Ain't Rocket Surgery

It Ain't Rocket Surgery: 21 Simple Tips that will Take Your Sales to the Moon!

All Rights Reserved

COPYRIGHT © 2021 Brian McKittrick

This book may not be reproduced, transmitted, or stored in whole or in part by any means, including graphic, electronic, or mechanical without the express written consent of the publisher except in the case of brief questions embodied in critical articles and reviews.

ISBN: 9798548993649

Imprint: Independently Published

Cover design by: Amber Castañeda

Edited by: Kathryn Tague

This book is dedicated to the memory of my father, John Arthur McKittrick (1950-2005).

Thank you for your unwavering support and dedication to family.

Table of Contents

FOREWORD I

INTRODUCTION: WHAT DOES IT MEAN TO BE A SALESPERSON? III

SECTION 1 - THE SALESPERSON 1

   CHAPTER 1 – THE PRE-APPROACH: GETTING READY TO SELL 3
   CHAPTER 2 – ZEAL: WHAT ARE YOU PASSIONATE ABOUT? 13
   CHAPTER 3 – VALUES AND YOUR MISSION: SHOULD YOU CHOOSE TO ACCEPT IT 23
   CHAPTER 4 – LIKABILITY: THE ATTRACTIVE CHARACTER 39
   CHAPTER 5 – TRAINING AND EDUCATION: BE A LIFELONG LEARNER 49
   CHAPTER 6 – HABITS: WE ARE WHAT WE REPEATEDLY DO 63
   CHAPTER 7 – YOUR BODY: THE MACHINE 75

SECTION 2 – THE SALES ENVIRONMENT 83

   CHAPTER 8 – GOALS: YOUR ROAD MAP TO ACCOMPLISHMENT 85
   CHAPTER 9 – FOCUS: POINT YOUR MIND IN THE RIGHT DIRECTION .. 97
   CHAPTER 10 – ALWAYS: DO WHAT WORKS EVERY TIME 105
   CHAPTER 11 – INNOVATION: CREATING SELLING SYSTEMS 113
   CHAPTER 12 – NICHES: WHO IS YOUR TARGET CUSTOMER? 127
   CHAPTER 13 – PROSPECTING: WHERE ARE TODAY'S BUYERS? 141
   CHAPTER 14 – DRESS THE PART: APPEARANCE MATTERS 157

SECTION 3 – THE SALES EXPERIENCE 167

   CHAPTER 15 – ENTHUSIASM: HAVING AN INFECTIOUS ENERGY 169
   CHAPTER 16 – THE BUILDING BLOCKS OF SALES 177
   CHAPTER 17 – VALUE: SELLING ON WHAT'S REALLY IMPORTANT .. 197
   CHAPTER 18 – OVERCOMING OBJECTIONS: THEY ARE REALLY BUYING SIGNALS 209
   CHAPTER 19 – THE CLOSE: HELPING THEM MAKE A DECISION 219
   CHAPTER 20 – WALK THE TALK: PRACTICING THE PRINCIPLES YOU HAVE LEARNED 233
   CHAPTER 21 – SCALING: GROWING YOUR BUSINESS EXPONENTIALLY 241
   CONCLUSION: SOME FINAL THOUGHTS ON THIS THING CALLED SALES 251

ACKNOWLEDGMENTS 259
ABOUT THE AUTHOR 263

It Ain't Rocket Surgery

21 Simple Tips that will Take Your Sales to the Moon!

Brian McKittrick

21 Simple Tips that will Take Your Sales to the Moon!

Foreword

It takes true leadership skills to organize a project of this magnitude. To you, it might just seem like just a sales book with a bunch of people's valuable input to start each chapter.

To get high caliber people to invest their time and energy into a project like this book is no easy feat. Brian has done a great job of cultivating inspiration from the right people, then he breaks down the right topics and in the right order.

I've been in sales my entire life. I've never had a job that didn't pay commission. I'm 41 years old now and if I could name one thing that's saved my life over and over again, it's the ability to sell.

I've used my sales skills to negotiate with gang leaders in prison, as well as negotiate with business tycoons on major investment deals. Every time I've fallen back in life, sales has been the rope that rescued me from the pit.

In my 25+ years of selling, I've watched countless people attempt the job and fail. My observation is that 100% of those who fail, overcomplicate the selling process and discount how powerful simplicity is.

For example, when I was selling mortgages in the early 2000s, I knew that my prospects didn't want a mortgage. They wanted a house and a payment from the mortgage was just a part of having it. While my counterparts in the office sold on rate, term, fees, and market corrections, I sold houses. Plain and simple. I never talked too much about rates, because rates didn't matter, the house did.

Brian McKittrick – It Ain't Rocket Surgery

This book simplifies sales, but most people will discount the power in these pages because of the fact that they tell themselves, "It can't be this simple/easy," but I'm here to tell you it can be and it is. The simpler you keep it, the more you sell.

My favorite saying is KISS: Keeping It Simple Sells

The easier it is for your prospect to make a decision, the more sales you will make. This book is dedicated to helping you simplify your sales process and close more deals as a direct result of it.

Lastly, don't be like the 99%. The 99% read a book, get the knowledge, and then don't do shit with it. Be the 1% that reads this book, takes action, and goes on to make millions in simplified sales.

Rise Above.

Ryan Stewman aka Hardcore Closer

21 Simple Tips that will Take Your Sales to the Moon!

Introduction: What does it mean to be a salesperson?

Brian McKittrick – It Ain't Rocket Surgery

21 Simple Tips that will Take Your Sales to the Moon!

"It's time to finally discover your inner badass, to live your best life, and to have the mindset to take on all that you wish. No more roadblocks, only progress, and success. The path to greatness begins with a single step."

Jenn Carrasco, Founder at V SkinCare Line, Speaker, and bestselling author of "Own Your Metabolism."

One of my all-time favorite quotes is the one below from Henry Ford:

"Whether you think you can, or think you can't, you're right."

Henry Ford (1863-1947), Founder of Ford Motor Company and chief developer of the assembly line technique of mass production

I've always loved this statement because it implies that mindset is the catalyst to our success in business. There is no shortage of amazingly talented people with poor self-confidence. And quite often, I've seen average talent succeed on the fuel of strong belief that they have no chance of failing. Despite what the average consumer thinks of the typical salesperson, sales is far from having a "gift of gab." It's more scientific and process with a stylistic art than some mystery skill that only a few suave personalities can pull off.

What does the word "sales" even mean?

Everyone has their own definition of the word "sales" or what it means to be a sales professional. I've heard it explained as: "Sales is the highest paying easy work you'll ever do!"

That's a true statement and nice sentiment if you are a sales champion, but what about the everyday salespeople? What about the guy or gal who's just getting going? What about the sales agent that is barely getting by and wants to do more? This book is for ANY sales professional who would like to take actionable steps to elevate their game.

If I were ever asked to define the word "sales," I would say this:

"Sales is guiding a prospective customer into the product or service that best fits their needs and budget, and encouraging them to buy it."

That's the simplest I've ever heard it expressed as to what a sales professional should be doing.

Whether you are in your first sales position or your fortieth, this book will help you. If you catch just ONE thing that you can add to your repertoire that leads to a deal, then reading this will have been worth your time. And realistically, my time as well. If you close a sale from something that you read here, you can tell ALL your friends and family about this book and how it helped you close that one deal that one time, which led to you winning a trip to Hawaii, which is where you conceived your daughter, who eventually went on to cure cancer. That's my hope for you, me, and humanity. You read - You sell - You tell others - They sell - I sell more books - Everyone is better off than where they started!

21 Simple Tips that will Take Your Sales to the Moon!

I fully believe that none of us are as smart as all of us, and sometimes, hearing information in a new way can inspire a change or light a fire of momentum that will carry you to new places. As you read this book, you may ask yourself, "Is it really that simple?" The answer will be a loud and resounding, "Yes!" Humans have a tendency to overcomplicate the mess out of nearly everything we do. We use nine words when five will do. We feel better to "think about it" when it's time for a new item to buy than to just act upon it, even though our mind was made up before we even got to the store. We research, then research, and research some more. I once had a client meeting with a lady on a health insurance plan, and she had almost filled a composition notebook with graphs, charts, and numbers. She was cross-referencing carriers, deductibles, copays, and premiums. In three questions, I was able to show her the EXACT plan she needed. But she spent who knows how many hours writing this all out.

The purpose of me writing this book is to give sales pros of all walks of life simple action items that can be done by anyone that will make an impact on growing their business. Whether you are a fantastic relationship builder that grows a book of residual clients, or you are in a transactional business model that is mostly single item sales, this book will give you pieces to add to your sales arsenal that can be implemented immediately.

But first…Who is Brian McKittrick, and why would you listen to him? Above all else, I am a man of convenience. I tend to see things in a simple way. Not that I don't analyze, because I absolutely do that when I am running reports. What I mean is that I can take data, and sometimes it's a massive amount, and boil it down to a simple concept. You could almost call me Captain Obvious.

Brian McKittrick – It Ain't Rocket Surgery

Wanna make more money in sales? Close more deals, duh!
Wanna close more deals? Get more leads, come on!
Wanna get more leads? Find more people who want to buy your stuff, of course!

I've taken this simple approach to sales since my first sales job; selling weed. Weed is marijuana for those who didn't grow up gangsta.

The problem that most 13-year-olds have when it comes to buying weed is that the folks to buy it from are not easy to find, and they are also very scary people to be around. But my friends and I liked to party, so we took the good with the bad. That lasted up until I was about 18. My friend Dustin and I realized one day that buying weed was way too hard. Why did it have to be so difficult, and why did everyone we knew that sold it have to act so tough? What if we went to a supplier, then became the go-to for our crew? We would be fun and easy to deal with, plus make some money as we go. So, we became: "Brian and Dustin - The Friendly Neighborhood Drug Dealers." I already had a pager and a Prime-Co cell phone. That's the old brick-sized phone with a retractable antenna (the commercial for the phone had the pink alien). For business cards, we wrote our pager's numbers in the margins of the face cards on a pack of playing cards. Folks that knew us would page us with "420," and we'd call them back from the cell phone.

We noticed a need in the marketplace, the need to be easy and fun when buying smoke. And it worked out very well for us. I think that was the catalyst of my sales career. My feeling is that, by and large, salespeople confuse the mess out of their prospects. I believe the reason I've been a top performer in any organization I've been a part of is that I always sought to make the process as easy as possible. As I said before, humans have a tendency to overcomplicate

21 Simple Tips that will Take Your Sales to the Moon!

things, and for the most part, prospects shop for a particular product or service to fill a need. As long as the right fit is presented and in the right price range, there is no need not to move forward. The mystery in sales is created by us.

Dustin and I did well. I'd get home from my job as a print pressman, get in the car after changing, pick him up, and then we'd hit the neighborhood. We'd get a page, call it back, then meet them wherever. The funny thing was since we were having such a good time, we'd hang out with them and smoke as we rode around. Our philosophy was to give them more value than anybody else was doing, so we came up with the idea of "fat sacks." Basically, it was the same bag everyone charged $25 for, but we only charged $20. Then, when we were hanging out, we'd smoked our stuff, so they wouldn't have to smoke what they just bought. That made our value proposition huge!

This all lasted until we had the realization that this was still a very criminal business. One day, I picked up our normal pound from our guy (who got his stuff directly from a Mexican connection), and it was not a square deal. That day I recognized that continuing on would require Dustin and me to carry guns, and that just didn't fit our motto.

What I learned from that experience stayed with me throughout my career.

- Be easy to work with
- Give the client more than what they paid for.
- And have fun.

The skills of sales translate to all industries. By breaking things down to their simplest form, they are far easier to understand and communicate with others. In dealing with customers and staff, the combination of simplicity, empathy, and confidence will be what's needed to perform. Keeping a simplicity mindset and not overcomplicating the process has led me to excel as a top-performing salesperson, sales manager, and entrepreneur over my twenty-plus year history. And that success has come in retail stores, car sales, and insurance brokerage.

Weren't you scared to be selling drugs?

One thing I want to address is fear. I can honestly say that at no time did I ever feel fear of either violence, theft, or being arrested. Seeing guns didn't bother me; rather, it was the realization that I would be asked to carry a gun in the future that I took as a warning that the drug trade was much more serious than how we were approaching it.

So, let's talk about fear for a moment. I'm one of four brothers (what would have been my older brother was stillborn in 1977, so effectively, I'm the oldest of three boys). I grew up in a poor household. My dad was a factory engineer, and my mom was a fast-food manager. The house was in very bad shape, and we had a roach infestation. We stretched every dollar. Our meals were cheap, and so were our clothes. Family outings were never to fancy places. Dining out was usually fast food or maybe a local diner. Vacations were camping instead of hotels. As kids, we chose to ignore most of how we were growing up because we still made it amazingly fun. But deep down, I knew we didn't have much. Things didn't get much better when - at 14 years old - my parents divorced. For one year, I lived with my mom and two brothers. But that didn't last because we had to downsize, unfortunately, to a place that only fit two teenage boys rather than three. I then moved in with my dad. I very much enjoyed living with my dad, because the two of us were very close. The downside was that my dad was trying to carry the mortgage on our house, his one-bedroom apartment that we shared, and pay child support. At 14, I had to go to work. It's very common for people to say that they worked their way through college, but I worked my way through high school. My dad was, at one point, an entrepreneur. But the pressure of having to provide for a family forced him to "get a real job" working for the plant in Fort Worth, General Dynamics, which is now Lockheed Martin. Up until his death at age 55, he worked for the plant to make sure his family had the basics covered. He would often tell me to get a good job with a salary and benefits so I could provide for my family. My dad would often advise this despite being laid off countless times or being forced to strike.

The very reason I bring this up is that I see every win as a major blessing. And at each stage of my career, a new level is set. My friend Kris Whitehead says, "Today's ceiling is tomorrow's floor." What that means is that every time you ascend to a new position or achieve a new goal, your base is now higher. Most of my sales career was commission retail. I spent one year in car sales, and at the end of 2015, I left retail store management to jump full-time into the insurance field. Early in my career, my goal was to earn $2,000 for every year of my age. I don't know where this came from, but it somehow became my barometer of success. And I achieved that each year. That changed when I made the move to commission insurance. The goals got far larger, and my horizon expanded. Moving into commission-only sales never scared me. I knew what it took to be a high-achieving store manager, and I could go back if I needed to. In insurance, I learned what it took to be a six-figure earning agent, then multiple six-figure earning team leader, then a seven-figure business owner. I learned what it takes to earn both as an agent and how to earn and scale as a business owner. As we step up to those new levels in our careers, we raise the floor of our abilities. Do not be afraid of taking a chance to pursue a new level. Once you have accomplished what you need to at the level you're on now; you now know what it takes to be successful in that role. As you ascend, the floor is being raised. What you are actually doing is minimizing the risk of failure in a new role or endeavor because even if the new venture didn't work out, you can go back to operating successfully in your previous position. You can succeed at the last level because you already know what it takes in order to achieve.

Where do we get confidence?

I see lots of cool graphics of inspirational quotes tied to amazing apex predator animals like lions, tigers, sharks, eagles, and so forth. I think these graphics are fantastic. However, what I think humans tend to forget is that we are unique.

We have the amazing gift of choice.
We have the amazing gift of communication.
We have the amazing gift to design our own lives.

Take inspiration from these terrible beasts and birds, but please remember that we are the ones made in God's own image and use that phenomenal power to enrich humanity.

Who is this book for?

We are going to look at 21 areas in which any sales professional can make an improvement. These are simple to understand, which makes them more easily implemented. This also means you have no excuse not to execute these strategies. When we simplify the approach, we take away the claim that it will be difficult to implement something new.

This book is for the salesperson who's just getting started.

21 Simple Tips that will Take Your Sales to the Moon!

This book is for the steady salesperson who feels like they have plateaued or needs a boost to take it to the next level. This book is for the top performers who are looking to scale their business.

This book is for the sales leader who wants to motivate and teach their team to excel.

This book is for the business owner who wants to replicate the sales success that got them to the top.

I say simple because when I talk about sales, "IT AIN'T ROCKET SURGERY!"

Let's take off!

21 Simple Tips that will Take Your Sales to the Moon!

Section 1 - The Salesperson

Brian McKittrick – It Ain't Rocket Surgery

21 Simple Tips that will Take Your Sales to the Moon!

Chapter 1 - The Pre-Approach: Getting Ready to Sell

Brian McKittrick – It Ain't Rocket Surgery

21 Simple Tips that will Take Your Sales to the Moon!

"Mindset is a result, not a starting point. Give yourself permission to be successful and allow all the abundance that you're currently working too hard to create and attract."

Stacy Raske, Army Veteran, star of TV's "4 Days to Save the World," and best-selling author of "Be a Boss and Fire That Bitch"

Purpose: In this chapter, we will be discussing the importance of preparing yourself and your environment before your prospects begin to arrive.

Before we begin to look at the actions and strategies for dealing with prospects and clients, we must first prepare ourselves, then prepare our environment. The single greatest investment you can make is the one in yourself. There is no other return on investment as high as the investment you put in learning and growing. It's hard to quantify personal growth, but after a while of working on you, when you step back and look at your progress, you'll be amazed to see how far you've come.

So, when I talk about pre-approach, I am discussing the preparation in both your mindset and in your environment before the customer sees an advertisement, visits a website, or walks onto your storefront.

Mindset

When you are in sales, you must decide on the answer to this question: Are you an order taker or an entrepreneur?

Maybe you're an entrepreneur and never realized it because you haven't started a new a business. Well, I hate to be the one to break the news to you; a sales professional is their own business! Every single sales pro is a walking and talking billboard of their own brand. So, consider yourself an entrepreneur, even if you work for another company, even if you have a salary base, even if you just started. You are in business for yourself. But in order to be a successful entrepreneur (or intrapreneur for those that are employed by someone else), you must begin to think of yourself as one.

Even a modest study of personality profiles will show you that being a true entrepreneur is made possible by your personality make-up. When you think like a true entrepreneur, there's a mindset that comes from four (4) ways of seeing the world:

- Removing of Doubt - Unwavering self-confidence
- Unique Thinking
- Adventurous Work
- Seeing a Big Picture

There are more components of being an entrepreneur, such as being a fierce competitor, wanting to be in control, and an overwhelming desire to do what others will not, and in most cases, dead sexy. I don't know what it is about sales that makes the folks as good-looking as they are. It's probably because many entrepreneurs hold their health in such high regard. Those that work hard at the office also tend to work hard at the gym, hence the hotness.

21 Simple Tips that will Take Your Sales to the Moon!

Removing Doubt - Unwavering self-confidence

Entrepreneurs have thick skin and hard heads, or so it may seem. This is because many of us have removed doubt from our brains. This absence of doubt is foundational to the way an entrepreneur operates. You don't hear, "This can't be done!" Instead, you will hear, "This is my idea. How do we get it done?" Ideas take courage to get going. Many of humanity's greatest accomplishments would never have come into existence if thoughts of fear or doubt had entered into the minds of the entrepreneurs that created them. An entrepreneur is more focused on winning, fame, glory, and profit, which overpowers doubt or the fear of failure. Entrepreneurs will evaluate risk but will not be deterred by it. Erase doubt, and let unwavering self-confidence lead you through all manner of challenges, problems, disasters, and glorious victories.

Unique Thinking

Entrepreneurs are action-driven people. Many of them do not enjoy digging into the small details of any project. The visionary types are absolutely great at starting anything, but it takes partnering with an integrator type for executing a project to completion. It's not because a visionary can't; it's just that new projects are more exciting, and the ideas are constantly flowing. Entrepreneurs will change the way things are done just because or to make them more efficient. They are adventurers, pioneers, and creative thinkers who have a result as their primary goal. Acting in the Present moment mindset, they have no fear and spend zero time thinking about yesterday. They know that TODAY is where it all happens; they will start early and finish late to get ahead of any schedule, timescale, or competitor.

Adventurous Work

If your "work" is an adventure, it's not really work. An entrepreneur's work is the adventure. The concept of real work is lost because the goal that is set out before them makes what an entrepreneur does so fun for them. The moment it begins to feel like work is when they staff someone for the position that requires "work." This is why you'll rarely find any real entrepreneur in an employee situation unless that position allows for a lot of leeway or creative license to be done their way. This is what is referred to as an intrapreneur. An entrepreneur has a hard time conforming to anyone else's rules. They don't like being told what to do. Rules can be tough to an entrepreneur because they are truly independent thinkers. Many entrepreneurs are labeled as having an obsessive-compulsive mindset or have even been described by family members as workaholics. That is not how entrepreneurs see themselves, but that is the frequent perception of outsiders.

Seeing a Big Picture

Entrepreneurs can be divided in two ways:

Visionary - seeing the big picture.
Integrator: filling in the picture

Some entrepreneurs are great planners, and others are great at executing the plan. Read the books "Rocket Fuel" and "Traction" by Gino Wickman. These will help you identify which talent you have and which role to play. A visionary type of entrepreneur will see a high-level view rather than have any kind of detailed plan or blueprint to follow. They might see business as if they will figure out the steps along the way. Planning more than a few steps ahead is pointless in their eyes. An integrator type will do much better to execute a plan that has been created, or at the very least, drafted, rather than let their intuition run free. But common to both will be the absence of doubt, and there will be controlled chaos.

Have any of these statements or qualities described you?

Working as an entrepreneur can be challenging. There will be a constant flow of new ideas, perspectives, and projects. Some projects may start without much planning, or you may have no time for waiting. Some projects require you to live in the now, which can be a struggle to understand where the direction of the goal is. This is why many entrepreneurs are solitary beings who can work very well on their own. Or they may be the leader of a team, but very rarely is an entrepreneur the member of a team. For entrepreneurs, the only rules they are interested in are those they make themselves. One major key to success as an entrepreneur is educating yourself. I commend you for reading this book. Being a good entrepreneur is a wonderful education; it's always fun and is very much like playing 'the accelerated game of life' every day. Whether you are an independent entrepreneur or an intrapreneur within a company, taking the viewpoint that your sales are your own company will make an enormous difference in how you handle your business and your success.

Environment:

What have you done to prepare for a customer?

This is a very important part of the sales process; however, it is the one most neglected. A customer's first impression of your store or office and the way you do business can be a great help or hindrance to closing a sale. You must make every effort to make your customers' initial impression a favorable one. Here are some of the things that customers use to form a judgment (good or bad) about you. Think about them from a sequence of your customer walking up to your business:

Condition of the parking lot
Signage lit up
Advertising up and looking good
Condition of building
Trash in the lot or around the door
Fingerprints on door
Attractive decorations
Ads prominently displayed
Dust on displays
Attractive displays
Salespeople standing around outside, or worse, smoking. Sorry folks, but it can turn some people off.
Hovering salespeople
Salespeople standing around talking to each other
How the staff is dressed and groomed
Body language and facial expressions
For online businesses, it is the quality of the ad we present, the layout of our landing page and website, and how easy it is to navigate.
The list goes on and on...

Please remember that ALL salespeople are business owners, whether it's your company or not. Even if you work for a company, your own clients are your business. Keeping that in mind, you must make every effort to make your customer's initial impression a favorable one. What we just listed are some of the areas that customers perceive to form a judgment (good or bad) about you.

Have you ever walked every step of your sales process?

21 Simple Tips that will Take Your Sales to the Moon!

This is the chance to literally go to the drawing board and examine each piece of your steps the customer must go through from their perspective.

How does it look?
How does it feel?
What steps do you put them through?
Can that be streamlined?

Simplicity and Efficiency make every sale easier. The best closing technique is to make every other step before the close as simple as possible. The fewer moving parts, the better chance you have to earn and keep a client.

There is a term we use in the Apex group called "Build Your Machine."

Building your machine is the process of constructing your business around your ideal client. Once you identify the specific avatar of who you want to work with the most and every aspect about them, you then simplify your process. The next step is to maximize the opportunities to reach your ideal prospects.

It is worth investing some time and examining how you and your organization are being perceived by your customer. The better the first impression, and then how easy your process is, will help in closing more sales and building a raving fan base.

Takeaways:

- **You need to prepare yourself mentally BEFORE you begin your sales process. Shift your viewpoint from that of just a salesperson to being a business owner; regardless of if you own the company or not, your clients are your business.**
- **Remove potentially negative impressions, so you're not starting off the sale with the prospects already having strikes against you.**

Statistic on Sales: 55% of the people making their living in sales don't have the right skills to be successful.

By changing your point of view to that of an entrepreneur, you will force yourself to be more engaged and want to improve your effectiveness.

Exercise: Mentally walk yourself through your sales steps. Take a viewpoint from the customer's lens.

Get your worksheets in the book resource page: book.itaintrocketsurgery.net

Chapter 2 – Zeal: What are you passionate about?

"When preparation and opportunity collide, it causes a seismic upheaval and that's how mountains of money are made!"

21 Simple Tips that will Take Your Sales to the Moon!

"Too many people doing stuff they don't wanna do to impress people they don't even like. You gotta define what success means to you because it's probably different for the next man."

Zach Babcock, Founder and Chief Visionary Officer at Podcast Powertrain and bestselling author of "Prison to Promised Land"

Purpose: In this chapter, we will look at tapping into our passion for living life and our purpose for working.

Live Your Life on Purpose and Get the Most out of Each Day

Have you ever felt like you are just moving throughout the day or just going through the motions?

Is it hard to separate the days, or does one day bleed into the next?

Have you been in a sales role for years and wondered where all the time has gone?

If this describes anything about you, then send a check or money order for $79.95 to "Wake Yo Ass Up" in Hoboken, NJ.

Just kidding about that last line. What's missing is having a passion and meaning in your life. When this happens, your days are not filled with routines; they become the necessary tasks to accomplish your goals.

Discovering your passion and purpose is paramount to enjoying our short time on this planet. I don't mean to get too deep into the weeds of the soul here, but I think it's vital to discuss what we are truly looking for in life. We all need something far beyond the next twenty-four hours that keeps us in an optimistic frame of mind during our day on the sales floor. It is positive for our joy and well-being. The problem we have as a society is that many people go right into work or a career without having gotten in touch with any sense of their passion and purpose. We tend to choose security in a paycheck and disregard the talents we have shown since childhood. Working hard is great, but working for money alone will not sustain you. We choose our careers to feel safe, despite what it does to our spiritually.

Humans have been in search of life's meaning ever since we were booted out of the Garden of Eden. I'm not addressing the esoteric meaning of life, but I am talking about the need to find your purpose or passion in your sales work life. Mankind is not designed to hump away for decades and allow life to pass by without really living it. If you never have, it's time to set some goals that will allow you to experience life outside your comfort zone. Find your passion and construct a life to support it. It most likely will not be possible to change your work immediately to something you love, but that paycheck can be used as a mechanism and provide a means to an end, and by following your passion, it will often lead you there. We might all have to start by earning money in ways that do not feed our soul, so how do you find what you are excited about that will lead to work-life fulfillment?

21 Simple Tips that will Take Your Sales to the Moon!

Finding Your Passion

Discover what is most important to you.

There is no guilt in finding what YOUR importance is. Growing up, many people are forced or pressured into a role that is not what they hold as significant. You need to truly dig what you hold significant. Your passion in life is within hidden in there somewhere.

Do you find pleasure in helping others or personal achievement?
Do you love competition?
What brings you the most joy and happiness?

Sometimes what we are working on today is a means to an end. We still must enjoy going to the office every day, but we can have our eye on something larger.

I have a friend of a friend named Dusty Black. Dusty is a country and western singer-songwriter, but it was only recently that he began to write and perform full-time. Dusty had been playing guitar and writing songs at an early age, but after school went into the workforce, starting as a mortgage broker in his twenties. The money was good but not scalable in mass. Dusty had the idea to start a moving company, one like the public had never seen. He had some experience in moving, and the reason he felt compelled to create a company was from seeing the piss-poor service most "professional" movers provided. Dusty's new company was Black Tie Moving. The company flourished in the space by being an elevated experience for their clients. This led to Dusty being an executive as the company grew and expanded. But through all these years, Dusty had never given up on his true passion for music. Once he had his moving company staffed properly, he was able to replace himself at the executive level and invest his time and energy into music full-time. His records have been a massive success, and his fame is rising. Dusty kept the fire for music alive and used the moving company as the means to the end that allowed him to step back into music. How can what you do today be the engine that drives your passion?

Imagine the short-term and long-term

What could you do right now, or in the next two years, that sounds exciting to you? Long-term goals can be more meaningful, but it is important to enjoy life in the present, too. These short-term purposes or targets are milestones on the way to achieving the big goal. Short-term accomplishments a lot of times can be taken care of in your "free time." I say that with quotes because time off the sales floor, in my opinion, can still be spent working toward a goal. For instance, watching a movie with your spouse is a positive step in building a strong(er) marriage. I am not in any way saying that you must be "on" all the time; I'm making the point to work and play with intention.

So, if you have a few hours or a Saturday to yourself, how would you choose to spend it?

Would you go visit someone important to you? Would you take time to learn? Or would you spend some time chilling out? There is nothing at all wrong with relaxing, but if you are just getting by through your workday and living for the weekend, you are not building a future to look forward to. You cannot complain about money if you are spending your free time watching TV or partying with friends. I know people who, during football season, will watch games all day Saturday and Sunday. It's hard to live a meaningful life if you're spending all your free time on the couch, mentally fixated only on being entertained. Choose your television programs at the proper times, but if you are working on a project, you will have very little time to waste. The average CEO spends 2 hours a day on "playtime," BUT at least half of that time is spent reading. You can find something better to do than watch TV or seeking to be entertained.

Long-term or even life-long pursuits are usually more profound and meaningful, therefore, are likely to require more time and energy. Many times, these are goals we want to accomplish before the end of our life, or maybe in the next ten or twenty years. This is where you would define your life's purpose or dream. Imagine if a doctor told you that you only have weeks left to live; what would be the one thing you wish you had done? If you had all the resources you needed and unlimited time every day, how would you choose to spend that time? A great exercise is to describe your perfect day. That description may very well be the pursuit your career will lead you to. Pursuing a major life goal is not much different in daily tasks from your shorter goals. The functionality is nearly identical; there just may be more steps in the process and require building a larger network or team.

Get out of your comfort zone

If you find yourself stuck in a rut, you can break out of it with a shake-up in your thinking by trying a new activity or taking in new information. Having new experiences helps to make the days unique and less likely to run together. If you are not sure of your purpose or want to create a more exciting life, set a goal to find your life's passion. Give yourself 30 days and spend a few minutes each morning and night to work on it. Get in a quiet space and close your eyes, or maybe take a walk, but listen for the answer. You can start by making a list, adding to it, then make an evaluation at the end of the month. Most of us are limited by our fear of failure or a fear of the unknown. However, the most meaningful activities are most likely outside of your comfort zone. You should have some goals in life that scare you in a good way. Your passion and purpose should be outside of the norm. It should be moving and exciting. Be brave enough to explore all your opportunities. The ones that are crazy enough to think they can change the world are the ones that actually do.

A Story:

For most of the time in my childhood and adolescent years, I had a very bad stuttering and stammering problem. A stutter is what Porky Pig does when he talks, but a stammer is when you have trouble first starting a sentence. For people that have this issue, it's usually words that start with hard consonants that are the trouble. In high school, I had many arguments with some folks who were less courteous about the issue, and let's just say I learned some skills in fisticuffs. I dealt with this into my early twenties, but one day in 2002, I had a chance to make a change. I was performing well as a salesman for a home electronics retailer, Ultimate Electronics, at the brand-new Frisco, Texas store. The area that I was excelling in was selling audio components and systems (those big speakers that audiophiles will put in their media rooms). I have been a pseudo musician since 1994, so music was a passion of mine, and I spoke very strongly in my presentations of audio products. I was consistently the top performer in the audio category. One day my store manager, David, approached me about giving a presentation at one of our Saturday sales meetings. I was truly nervous. I hadn't ever spoken in front of anyone before. I was excited to be recognized and loved the idea of teaching the group, but I couldn't get over the worry of my speech issues. David told me the fix, and this works whether you have a problem with speaking or not. When you are given a chance to speak or make a presentation, if you have notes or an outline, this will help you stay on track. It also will show the audience

21 Simple Tips that will Take Your Sales to the Moon!

that you are prepared, have an agenda, and are knowledgeable in their eyes. For me, having an outline helped me not to have to think about where I was going because I already had a map for my talk. I also had the ability to read bullet points from the page and then elaborate. I wouldn't stammer when I was reading, so this made my presentation seem to me, mentally, that I was reading. And the last benefit was that it helped me to slow down, and that also helped me to not fumble over my words.

I could have easily told David that I didn't want to do the training, and he probably would have relented, but being willing to try something that sounded exciting to me, it helped me to overcome a problem I had experienced my whole life. These days, I no longer stutter or have to think of what I am going to say. That lead me to do presentations all the time as a salesman, then be comfortable giving sales meetings, which has led to having a training business and now writing this book. You never know what stepping outside your comfort zone will do for you.

Are you ready?

Ready to tap into your passion?
Ready to turn your back on average?
Ready to make a new (or renewed) commitment?

I first started speaking and conducting trainings in 2003 at age twenty-three. Eighteen years later, I'm writing this book. It's never too late, and age doesn't make a difference for anything.

"You don't have to be great to start, but you gotta start to be great." – Zig Ziglar

Takeaways:

- Look inward to find areas you are passionate about. Set short-term and long-term targets around your passions. These don't have to be life-changing, but they can be.
- Be willing to try new things that you have been putting off because of fear.

Sales Statistic: One in four salespeople majored in business. The second most popular major? The degree of life. 17% never attended college.

In many ways, life will teach us much more than what formal education can. Our purpose and passion can be drawn from our life experience, and the pursuits we hold in our hearts have been inspired by how life has shaped us.

Exercise: Write out a wild idea list of anything you want to be, do, or have. Make note of what stands out as the areas you get the most excited about.

**Access your book study materials at:
book.itaintrocketsurgery.net**

21 Simple Tips that will Take Your Sales to the Moon!

Chapter 3 –Values and Your Mission: Should you choose to accept it

"It's not a great mission statement, but we'll revise it if things get better."

21 Simple Tips that will Take Your Sales to the Moon!

"Part of the problem with new small business owners and entrepreneurs is that they don't take the time to structure their core values and just jump right in. The beautiful part about using core values within your business is that there is no right or wrong way to do it."

- Tomas Keenan, COO of Break Free Academy and bestselling author of "Unf*ck Your Business"

Purpose: In this chapter, we will be talking about defining your core values, vision, and personal mission statement

You may have heard the term "Moral Compass." The meaning is to have an internal guide of values that directs us in our efforts and areas of interest. It's incredibly important and useful for knowing your values. Knowing your values will give you clarity and focus, and values can be used to define your priorities. Clearly defined priorities can determine how to best spend your time and energy. So, establishing a set of values can actually make decisions come easier, and this will help streamline your business.

You may be wondering why this might be relevant in a sales book. Having a set of core values you live and work by will guide you in how you sell and who you sell to. If any part of your sales role is not congruent with your values, you must either change that part or change your role.

The process here is to: define your values, articulate a vision, and then create a mission statement to clarify the focus of the organization.

Defining Your Values

It's incredibly important to set your own principles to have a floor from which to stand firm in your beliefs. To do this, you must truly know yourself. It's easy to get distracted by the ideals of others and take them as your own because of certain pressures, but to create a set of life and business values, you must get in touch with your own morals. Your values, simplified, are the things that are most important to you. They are unchangeable beliefs in what you stand for. When you know you have your values down, you can construct a simple pattern of doing what's most important to you.

Identifying your values is looking inward and deciding who you are and who you want to be. This may take some time to evaluate and require imagining your future self. Take some time to reflect on all the different areas of your life, establishing what is most important to you and what your life goals are. These answers will help you establish your values.

It's very important that these values are YOUR values. It's unfortunate that many of us are working to achieve the goals someone else gave us. In my lifetime, I've seen this with folks that become doctors and lawyers because a parent, or parents, applied such immense pressure for them to do so. This may be painful, but you will never be happy working on another person's pursuits.

You can make a list of as many values as you consider important. The key is to set which ones are your highest priorities. This will make sure you are working at the most important parts of your life. How would you know if you are making progress if you haven't decided where you're going? This is your chance to define and articulate as many values in your life as you see important.

If you are not sure where to start, below are some main categories:

Creativity

Not everyone is a Mozart or Michelangelo, but we all have the ability to express ourselves creatively in our work and business life. You can utilize creativity in sales any day of the week. The world needs it. Merchandising in retail stores. Design in your sales marketing funnel. Try thinking outside the box while you're on the sales floor.

Faith

Few areas of life occupy more of our values than our faith. Faith is the part of our makeup that requires belief in the unseen and unknown. It is an absolute must to establish your values of faith. I am not using this book to advocate any religion. There are many non-religious value systems as well. You may find great enjoyment by spending time studying and finding your spirituality.

Friends and Family

Valuing relationships includes fostering all relationships of importance; in addition to your romantic ones, family can also mean your close ones of choice. Those are your associates you are choosing to do life with. Having value in family means that you hold your time and activity with your loved ones to be extremely important. In order to strengthen this value, spend quality time and effort on building relationships.

Fitness

We discuss fitness more in chapter 7, but you must decide how much of an importance in your life you take your health. Your body may be the one part of life that is hard to fix if you have abused it for too long. It does not make sense to earn a substantial living but be too out of shape to enjoy it in retirement.

Finance

People that say money isn't important to them will lie about other things too. Whatever goal you decide to set for yourself, just realize that the higher the goal, the more effort you must apply, and the scale of effort magnifies as you increase your income levels.

Legacy

So many of us are concerned only about the next step in our journey that we forget about living an everlasting impactful life. If asked about legacy, most people will say that they just want others to have a fond memory of them. There are countless ways that you can make your mark on the world if that's important to you. Choose to pursue a legacy of how you can be a positive influence on others.

Take time to make your list of highest priority values. As an example, my business values list is below:

- T – Trustworthy - We do the right thing at all times and keep our word.
- E – Enthusiasm - We go all-in with energy and fun!

- A – Achievement - We push ourselves to achieve our goals, no matter what the challenge is.
- M - Making a Difference - We pursue difference-making work to impact our community and the world.
- S – Simplicity - We keep our actions and communication simple, so everyone can follow along.

This creates the acronym TEAMS. Each segment of a company is a team. And if you think about it, a family is also a team. And that is extremely important to me.

Use your values list to make sure you have chosen the right sales organization. Does your current company line up with your values? If not, should you consider making a change? Now I am not advocating for jumping ship to a new place, but if you are not aligned, there will be friction to deal with. It is not possible to be emotionally fulfilled if you are out of sync in your current role.

Using the attributes in this list will give you the structure of a proper values list.

Having Clearly Articulated Values Streamlines Decision-Making

We all are faced with tough decisions. There is very little we can do to avoid the need to make tough decisions. But you can make them easier. By defining your values and putting them to practice in your daily life, you will be able to make decisions easier and more quickly. Life has more clarity when you are clear about living with your values, and when presented with a choice, the best option is more obvious. You can avoid unneeded stress by allowing your values to be the filter you run all tough decisions through.

In developing your list of values, remember these benefits:

Your values become your moral compass, if you will, very much like your conscience. Your conscience has been developed and trained over time so that you know right from wrong. This may have come from experiences, formal education, or mentorship. The same thing applies to your values. By sticking to your values as your moral compass, you will find the process much simpler when faced with a tough decision. Choose values that you know will guide you well.

You can take comfort knowing that your values have kept you in line. This is a huge load of weight from stress off your shoulders! Most of the stress we put on ourselves comes from worry. If you consistently are acting out of lines from your values, you will be putting unnecessary burden on yourself. On the other hand, if at the end of the day you acted completely in line with your values and character, you will rest easy with a clear head.

You will have the respect of your friends, family, and colleagues. Respect of our peers is very important to our psyche. It confirms to us that what we are doing is right, and we are on the right track. When you operate within your values, others will take notice. They see you as a person guided by your own morals and not shaken by the outside world. Over a period of time, two actions will take place. 1. You will attract positive people to your life that appreciate your integrity. 2. You will push away the negative people from your life who don't align with your values. Both of these actions come from the basis of respect. Even if someone doesn't agree with your values and morals, as long as they are positive and constructive values, they will respect your integrity by sticking to them.

21 Simple Tips that will Take Your Sales to the Moon!

Values can impact your interactions and responses to loved ones. You can avoid giving in to the pressure from those close to you by adhering to your values. By blocking out what doesn't align with your values, you will avoid being subjective to the mumbo-jumbo around you that might normally influence you. If they truly care for you, they will respect your value position.

I could list many more benefits of outlining a values list, but what's most important here is to align your actions with your values through values-based decision-making.

Vision

Once you have your values clearly defined, the next step is to create a vision of your ideal personal and professional path. This becomes the map, if you will, describing where you are going. In order to achieve big things in your life, you must be willing to think big. You should dream big and envision your goals to make them happen. Achieving your targets and goals is best achieved when you can imagine every detail of what it is you want to achieve.

A fantastic book on vision called "Full Steam Ahead! Unleash the Power of Vision in Your Work and Your Life" was written by Ken Blanchard and Jesse Stoner. In that book, Blanchard and Stoner enumerate eight (8) elements of a compelling vision:

1. Helps us understand what business we're really in
2. Provides guidelines that help us make daily decisions
3. Provides a picture of the desired future that we can actually see
4. Is enduring

5. Is about being "great"—not expressed solely in numbers
6. Touches the hearts and spirits of everyone
7. Helps each person see how he or she can contribute

Tips on developing your vision

Find a quiet spot to take time to imagine what your future holds. What does your life look like next year, in five years, ten years, then beyond? Think as far ahead as you would like. Include all aspects of your life in as minute detail as you can. Create a vivid mental picture of what you would want to be in the future, thinking of each detail that comes to mind.

As you make clear visual pictures that you are passionate about, begin to write them down or otherwise make a record of them. Take note of as much detail as you can put in the description. It's a good idea to keep your mood and feelings in mind. Positive feelings will build excitement about your vision.

Watch out for possible distractions. Some vision items may not align with your core values or your purpose from Chapter two. Learn from past mistakes of times you lost focus from your main priorities and what lead up to your attention being diverted.

Many people use a vision board to create a space that gives them pictures of their goals. This can be clips from publications or images printed off the web. Commonly, you will see vision boards with inspirational phrases that support your visions. Vision boards are very effective by being displayed in a high traffic area that gives you a moment to remind you of your goals throughout the day.

21 Simple Tips that will Take Your Sales to the Moon!

Are you in the right place? It may be something heavy to think about, but are you in the right location? This is a question from the viewpoint of your business space and even the town you are living in. It may not be feasible to move right away or even in the near future, but if you are better suited mentally to be in a different environment, then you must consider it.

Your life vision should be a very high priority. If you are to turn your visions into a reality, you must commit time each day to work on them. Consider your vision when making the next moves in your personal and business journey.

Writing Your Own Personal Mission Statement

Now that you have outlined your values and crafted a vision, the next thing is to use those to write your mission statement. What is your mission? Most people have no idea how to answer that question and become a wandering generality, just making their way through each day without much priority other than paying their monthly bills. Maybe you don't have an answer to that question because you've never considered it. That's unfortunate. Companies write mission statements, but we, as individuals, should look at creating one for our lives. Having a mission statement will actually help you make the best plans and decisions for your life's purpose.

What makes up a mission statement?

Components of a Mission Statement:

It's long-lasting: Your mission should be legacy, and something everlasting
It's customer-centric: Your mission should be about clients

It's ongoing: Your mission should have energy and always be building.
It's a big deal: Your mission should be inspirational and have a huge impact
It's simplistic: Your mission should be easily communicated

How To Develop a Mission Statement

Outlining your mission is one of the keys to your own personal development and motivation, which guides your success, and leads to more fulfillment in your daily endeavors. By having a large target or destination in mind, it makes it easier to get through the daily challenges on the sales floor. A mentor of mine frequently quotes a friend of his by saying, "The big stuff makes you rich, but wealth is made in doing the mundane activities every day with focus."

Writing your mission statement

1. In chapter two, we talked about finding your purpose. Did you work on that? Most people have no idea what their purpose is because they most likely have never stopped to consider it. And that's a very sad thing. But by virtue of investing your time and money in this book, you are not like the average person. You're on your way to being a sales astronaut!

Take inspiration from your heroes. When we look up to others, we pick up on the parts of their lives that have most impressed or inspired us. I am not advocating for copying the life of someone else. One of the most destructive things we can do in our self-development is to compare our progress to others. My suggestion is to take note of positive attributes you admire in others. You can learn a lot from watching mentors in your sales or business field. The individuals in the trenches with you, doing the work, see the

21 Simple Tips that will Take Your Sales to the Moon!

intimate part of the daily routine. They also may be able accessible to speak with you one on one or be a paid mentor.

Some of the influencers on your mission may be celebrities or high-profile executives. If they are making an impact on the national level, chances are they will have a positive message. Take those into account as well.

Think long-term. Picture yourself at the end of your time on this "third rock from the sun." This would not be the time you'd want to have regrets. In most cases, regrets are for what we did NOT do in life. At that time, what would you have wanted to accomplish? What would be your legacy? Does that change your mission?

Get to work. The toughest part is just starting. We spend so much time strategizing and planning but putting off action. This is from a place of fear. Fear of getting it wrong, fear of failure, or for some, fear of success. Yes, that is a thing that some entrepreneurs experience.

It's time to write out your mission statement. You have all the info at this point. You want to keep it concise to the essential element, also something that is easy to remember and effectively articulates your overarching mission to accomplish. Don't feel locked in because you can make adjustments later.

You can tweak the mission statement over a period of time. Your mission may evolve over a period of time. It may not be helpful to constantly change your target, but you can refine your mission in the beginning before you settle on a statement that encompasses what you are pursuing.

How to Apply Mission Statements as a Professional Intrapreneur

An intrapreneur is a professional within a company that has some leeway to operate your own business within a company framework.

Reword your job description to align with your mission. If you developed your own mission, see how that aligns with your job role. This may adjust some of the tasks within your daily work. This could also help your approach in the office to give it greater purpose knowing the part it plays in your overall mission and goals.

Work with management. Make sure both parties are on the same page. Most organizations dream of this level of initiative from their sales staff to line up your mission within the company's guidelines. This will be greatly appreciated, but you must also keep in mind that you will still need to learn from sources outside your company. Be mindful if what is important to you is not important to your company. This may require some deep evaluation to determine if you are still properly in tune with your company.

Having your own mission statement will allow clarity in how you handle your business, both as an individual sales producer or as an intrapreneur within an organization.

21 Simple Tips that will Take Your Sales to the Moon!

Takeaways:

- **The process is to: articulate your values – conceptualize your vision – define your mission statement. By diligently working toward bringing your vision of life to fruition, you will be happier in your daily activity and find fulfillment in your journey. You will feel more passion and optimism in your daily life once you developed a clear vision.**
- **Visualizing the picture of your dream version of yourself is an excellent way to bring achieving your goals to the forefront of your mind and to determine what is most important to you.**

Sales Statistic: Top sales pros outperform low performers by 10:1 and average ones by 2:1.

Average is nothing to aspire to. And your only true competition is the person you see in the mirror. Having a grand vision of accomplishment and a mission to achieve it will create a map of your success.

Exercise: Take time to write out your own values, vision, and personal mission statement

The guide to assist you is located at book.itaintrocketsurgery.net

Chapter 4 - Likability: The Attractive Character

"I just got promoted again. It's easy to succeed if everyone likes you!"

21 Simple Tips that will Take Your Sales to the Moon!

> *"People want to be around and do business with interesting people. Even if you have an off the wall oddball thing that you love, it still makes you interesting. When you talk about it, people can feel your positive energy. And everyone loves a person with positive energy."*
>
> Jessica Stroud, Owner Midwest Insurance Solutions and bestselling author of "The Lady CEO"

Purpose: In this chapter, I will show you the steps to construct a likable character profile

Crafting the Attractive Character and Becoming More Likable

In numerous ways, you yourself are a marketing machine, a walking and talking billboard, if you will. Your personal interactions tell a story that those around you will remember. The posts you make on social media are mini-commercials that will stick in the minds of your followers over time. You can craft a persona by having a clear and consistent message that resonates with your audience. And that audience should be made up of your perfect (or dream) clients. The messages you create should be speaking directly to your ideal client. The way you communicate and carry yourself in person should be the professional your client wants to do business with. This is called an Attractive Character.

But how do you create the Attractive Character?

You be you, but you do it with almost maniacal consistency and simplicity. You are essentially the person you want to be around.

The most common mistake I see when I watch salespeople working on their image is when they try to copy the behavior and speech patterns of an influential person. If that person of influence is edgy, the salesperson will try to turn up their edginess. If the person of influence is passionate and motivating, the salesperson will attempt to speak like a self-help guru. The key is to take inventory of yourself and speak in your own words and style. When that happens, your authenticity will attract the type of clients you want to serve.

The first step is to evaluate yourself. You are far more interesting than you give yourself credit for. Make a list about you, and this can become the basis of what you put out in the public space. If you are posting on social media, this is the content most of the public is looking for when visiting social media platforms. Post more about these categories than anything else:

What do you do outside the office or in your spare time?

What are your hobbies?
The less common they are, the more interesting they will be.

What do you do for entertainment?
This will be music, movies, TV, art, and other attractions.

What books do you read?
This could be of any topic, and if you are into book series with a cult-like following, you'll attract those fans.

21 Simple Tips that will Take Your Sales to the Moon!

Do you have pets or work with animals?

How do you spend your family time?
Posting about family activities on social media, or even talking about family in conversation, is a huge bonding experience with your audience.

What do you talk about with your friends and coworkers?
Current events and news. These can be great conversation starters, especially if something local is a hot topic.

Money matters. This is a topic far too few people discuss in detail. Your product or service may involve money but be careful not to give tax or financial advice if you are not licensed for it.

Sports. What's the current team up to? You can bond quickly with other fans of the same team or even have some fun banter if they are fans of a rival team. As a lifelong Dallas Cowboys fan, I don't ever pass up a chance to have some friendly jabs at Philadelphia Eagles fans.

I usually avoid discussions on religion and politics with clients and prospects. It tends to be heavily emotional, but if you feel you can bond with your ideal client in these areas, then go ahead. I would just feel folks out and ease into the conversation. In my business, a person's religious and political views are irrelevant, so I don't bring them up.

Now for the business side. What's interesting about your job? And that answer can't be, "Nothing." All jobs solve a problem, fulfill a need, provide a service, or is the dream coming true for someone's wants. Do not take what you sell for granted. You need to regularly communicate the answers to these questions:

What problem does your product or service solve?

What clientele thinks it's sexy, awesome, or interesting?
Who could not live with the product or service you offered?

The single best way I have found to speak publicly or post about my sales role is to tell a story about my service overcoming a challenge a client was having. In my experience, this has been the best way to boast about my service without coming across as being a salesman. When you do this, you are expressing yourself as an expert, sharing positive benefits of your product or service, and relating to a prospect that might be having a similar experience.

Now that we have discussed how to share our attractive characteristics, let's talk about coming across as more likable in our personal interactions. These are merely tips. I am not advocating you try to fake being likable. Being insincere can be noticed from a mile away. What I am talking about is interacting with your prospects in a more likable manner.

For some people, being likable is a natural gift. We all know someone that everyone just seems to like. It's a wonderful feeling when people are happy to see us. Your social life is more enjoyable, and others are more willing to be helpful to the people they like. But being likable is actually a skill we can develop.

Common characteristics of highly likable people:

Being empathetic

The ability to understand another's feelings and point of view is priceless. One of the most frustrating times we experience as people are when others fail to understand what we're thinking and feeling. Be that person that makes the time and effort to get to the heart of the matter. Letting a prospect tell their story is invaluable, especially when you are the only one listening.

Being interesting

Unless there was a recent tornado or hurricane, stop talking about the weather! Get down to some real-deal stuff. People want to be fascinated and entertained. Speaking about the same boring topics everyone else is talking about won't get you invited to more parties. The easiest way to have interesting conversations is to talk about the interesting parts of your life. If you are bored with yourself, then you're probably boring others, too. Go have an adventure, then tell people about it.

Focusing on the positive

Most people don't like being around others that find negativity in all situations. Being negative and pessimistic becomes tiresome, even to other negative people. Remember that Saturday Night Live skit with Rachel Dratch called "Debbie Downer"? All her friends would leave after a while because she mentioned only the worst of everything they talked about. Most people like positive and happy people. Folks around you are affected by your words, actions, and moods. If you can make others feel good, they'll associate those positive feelings with you.

Being in the present

An area of increasing difficulty is to be truly present in the moment. You can quickly make someone feel insignificant by failing to give them your full attention. In sales conversations, avoid distractions, and keep your eyes and/or ears on the other person. We are becoming more distracted, making it harder to listen to what is being said. But we must be present, and anything else is rude and unappreciated.

Being confident

Allow yourself to be confident but not arrogant. Almost everyone likes to be around those who are confident. People that have a nervous and uncomfortable nature tend to make others uncomfortable as well. Work to find a piece of confidence that is just between arrogance and self-doubt. Holding a strong vision of your talents, being proud of your accomplishments, and believing in what you have to offer the world will make it possible to feel good about yourself and your abilities.

Keeping your word

If you cannot be trusted, then it makes it difficult for people to like you. Being honest and reliable creates the kind of trust necessary to build and sustain meaningful client relationships. Integrity is the basis of trust, and that is doing what you say you're going to do. If something comes up that prevents you from fulfilling your word, communicate that as soon as possible, and provide a resolution.

Keeping opinions to yourself (unless asked)

When people share their challenges, they already know what to do 90% of the time. In many cases, they're just looking for someone to listen and be sympathetic. Unsolicited advice is rarely welcome. The best case is to just ask if they are looking for feedback or just want to vent. Give advice only when requested. Otherwise, your opinion may be unwarranted.

21 Simple Tips that will Take Your Sales to the Moon!

Remembering names

We all feel a small bit of pride when others remember and use our names. It makes us feel important. It's also a little insulting when they don't remember our name. If someone has ever greeted you with, "Hey Guy!" then they don't know your name. For many people, names are among the most challenging things to remember about a person. People tend to remember more of a visual characteristic. You will just have to break this habit. Someone's name is one of the most important words to them. Do whatever is necessary to remember names and then use them in the conversation. You will be appreciated for it.

Making others feel good about themselves

You may think that being more likable is the result of being more impressive to others. That's not the case. It's actually about making people feel more impressed with themselves. Most people don't often think that they are doing very well. If you can make someone feel better about their own life and who they are, you'll build a warm spot within them, and you may have found a friend for life.

Never underestimate the tremendous power of being liked. But you must be yourself. These are small changes to make so you can develop the qualities that draw others to you and make others feel good about themselves.

Takeaways:

- **You're more interesting than you may be giving yourself credit for. What's special about you that you can promote to your audience?**
- **What areas of commonality do you have with your client that can be the basis of building rapport?**

Sales Statistic: 92% of consumers trust referrals from people they know.

Although this statistic is referring to the referral from a client to a friend, to me, this just emphasizes the need to get to know your prospect, and have them feel like they know you. You're just building trust by showing them you are a real person.

Exercise: Construct your character profile. What areas of being more open and likable are you needing to improve?

**The chapter guide is available at:
book.itaintrocketsurgery.net**

Chapter 5 – Training and Education: Be a lifelong learner

"It's the most effective motivation book I've ever read. It's a scrapbook filled with orthodontist bills, student loan bills, insurance bills, credit card bills, daycare bills..."

21 Simple Tips that will Take Your Sales to the Moon!

"Training is the one thing that every CEO acknowledges their employees need, but only a fraction of small business leaders make the time and investment to provide it. Training and professional development elevates employee engagement and job performance. It's a company's #2 asset, next to their people. Without it, companies will struggle to get the people-side of their business right."

Brenda Neckvatal, the HR Lady, International award-winning HR Pro and Best Selling Author of "Best Practices in Human Resources"

Purpose: In this chapter, we will look at the importance of learning at training and education events and how to capitalize on what you have learned.

Boost Your Sales Through Sales Training

One mega-powerful way to boost your sales is through training. One of the beautiful things about sales is that, if done properly, sales positions are the most effective way of earning unlimited income. The vast majority of salespeople, when asked why they preferred sales as their job, stated that in sales, they can earn income on tap. This proves that sales professionals have the choice to either earn more or earn less. Keeping that in mind, success in sales can have a dependence on the quality of sales training they have had. No one can claim to be an expert without the proper training and experience. And since you can't speed up experience, the best way to grow your expertise is to attend or consume or sales training.

Many salespeople are now more willing to get their rear-ends in more seats at seminars or have been seen stalking the business section at Barnes and Noble. The sharp sales pros know that improving sales skills and knowledge is one of the best ways to earn more and ramp up their success. Even prior to the pandemic forced folks to stay at home more, Research and Markets* had estimated that the online education market will hit $325 billion in revenue by the year 2025. While that number includes education for K-12 and online universities, more and more trainings are being created digitally. This is very exciting to me, and I hope it's something you take advantage of for your own benefit.

Quick Note: Take advantage of the social media ads you see for a "Free Book." You will find some great titles, plus it also gives you a chance to see how the proper sales funnel works.

If you have never understood why consistent sales training is as important as it is to your sales career, here are some advantages of corporate training, courses, or seminars:

It Sharpens Skills

The ability of a sales pro to build a strong book of business and close more sales is advanced through picking up more advanced sales and marketing strategies. Based on this basic concept, sales training is specifically created to help salespeople sharpen their skills and improve their craft.

21 Simple Tips that will Take Your Sales to the Moon!

It Boosts Attitude

Another great thing about sales training is that they do not only focus on improving the skills and abilities of the salesperson. Many seminars are a mix of mindset and tactical skill sessions. Through these events, the attitude and behavior of the salesperson towards their prospects and clients are improved. Topics like these are not going to be taught in the typical carrier and vendor training programs that usually only cover the features and benefits of products and services.

You'll Learn to Interact

Through the proper sales training, the sales folks will become better able to identify the right strategy in dealing with prospects and clients. Many courses will provide the right combination of language, perception, attitude, and the art of selling in order to generate business more efficiently. Sales training will teach salespeople how to deal with clients properly, how to handle objections and the art of persuasion. These activities make the seller realize that selling should never be hard, or what most salespeople believe is hard selling. The point here is that with proper interaction, selling becomes an art, where logic and emotion are used in combination to assist the client with buying.

You'll Add to Your Network

Meeting other salespersons at a seminar is a huge benefit for attending. It's almost as valuable as the content of the speakers. I have been to many conferences, and it's commonly said that interacting with other industry professionals is what the attendees mainly look forward to. The key here is to go into the event with the intention to add value. Do not be a taker. Look for ways to give, and you will be incredibly popular. The ones that go in looking for ways to serve themselves only will find few friends. Building a large network will allow you to share leads as referrals in industries that relate to your offering. Givers gain, so look to make as many connections as you can for sharing contacts.

If you have attended an effective sales training (like one of mine, wink-wink), then there's a very good chance you have acquired a new skill, tip, or tactic to grow your sales. Alas, most trainings are ineffective or the same mundane content that you're heard a ton of times, so most sales pros don't get overly excited to go to a sales meeting or training. If you have no benefit, then you don't have an interest. This also applies to the standard onboarding process with new sales staff.

One of the reasons many trainings don't add much value is the lack of communication or miscommunication. Without proper orientation on the sales job and proper understanding of the nature of the position, both the management and the employees will have a higher difficulty in understanding each other, and this will severely impact performance. The ability to share correct ideas and concepts is paramount to the success of the sales organization. So, the basis of all strong sales teams is quality training and education.

Without quality sales training, salespeople will be less confident in presenting their products. This is because they are not fully aware of how to face their clients and how to work through the sales process and set up their clients for buying. Another trouble of poor or no sales training is that without proper sales trainings, sales professionals will not be motivated to pursue a higher level. The vast majority of salespeople will sell just enough to get by or get satisfied in the comfort of their current position. This may be because

21 Simple Tips that will Take Your Sales to the Moon!

they don't feel they have the skills to close more deals or the knowledge level to become a leader in the organization.

Sales trainings should not be just any ordinary program, nor should a program be designed just for the sake of having it. Trainings must have a purpose, and the results should be to increase performance and income.

All great salespeople will look for ways to learn more about their craft or to maintain a positive mental attitude. But how do you pick the right training for you?

Start by addressing the gaps in your game or selecting areas you want to strengthen.

One of the most common mistakes is that individuals feel that they must spend time working to correct weaknesses, but the biggest results are seen when we maximize on our strengths. Unless you have a weakness that has become a detriment to your performance, you will gain more ground by making improvements to what you're already doing well.

List five (5) skills you possess in your life that are strengths to maximize or areas you feel lack discipline or direction:

- I excel at:
- I am solid at:
- I am inconsistent at:
- I am struggling with:
- I'd love to explore:

Next, you will want to find influencers in the areas in which you want to learn. There are also plenty of fantastic online courses to support new skills. Mastermind groups are also fantastic for learning, but also, they can help accelerate your growth by being around other like-minded people. Don't sleep on the events either. The attendees of business and sales seminars are making investments in themselves. These are the kinds of business men and women you want to be networking with.

Once you find the speakers and mastermind groups that you like, take the content very seriously and do the work. The biggest mistake you can make is not taking advantage of the materials. Not all of the business instruction and consulting are the same, but there is a lot you can learn as long as you take the time to dive a little deeper.

A key skill in capitalizing on training sessions is to be a good listener - then an action-taker.

Improving your listening skills is really important for being a top performer in sales and leadership. Listening is perhaps the better half of all communication. It's not very common for most people to have received any formal training on proper listening. But improving your listening skills will enhance your professional and personal life. Let's discuss some practical ways towards becoming a better listener, even in tough situations.

The Importance of Listening Skills

Mastering listening is an important part of communication. What you say is only one side of the conversation. We must take time to fully understand the messages that people are sending us and intently hear what they are saying. Truly listening is critical to showing prospects you value and appreciate what they are saying. Many misunderstandings and conflicts can be minimized if we were working to understand each other's viewpoints. This builds stronger relationships. Active listening will also help clarify expectations and priorities in an employee and employer role. This is paramount to make the best use of your time on the sales floor. Each side needs to express a sincere interest in what each other has to say and is crucial to quality interpersonal relationships.

Active listening can lead to increased mental and emotional health. Actively listening requires minimizing distractions. That means giving the speaker your full attention. While listening, if you notice yourself starting to wander in your mind, bring it back to the subject you should be focusing on. Making eye contact with the speaker can make a world of difference. It lets the speaker know you're interested and makes it harder for your mind to wander. If you are speaking with prospects over the phone, attempt to remove as many distractions as possible. A key for me is to stare blankly out the window. If that is not possible for you, find a blank space to cast your viewpoint. By doing this, you will avoid unnecessary stimuli that could take away your concentration. Being able to fully listen will also help you to empathize with others, which is powerful in improving your emotional health and enhance your own peace of mind.

Sometimes active listening is not easy, and that's okay. We want to encourage people to express themselves, even when people are hesitant to approach a sensitive topic. This is when we need to develop our empathy, and the best way to understand what a person is really communicating is to attempt to put yourself in their situation. If you use open-ended questions and patient pause when necessary, this will enable more open discussion. Actively try to understand their thinking process, and a best you can, what they are feeling. Many times, when we are having tough discussions, it evokes strong emotions, and it's tempting to react with our own feelings. You may need to detach yourself temporarily from your feelings. It's very important to distinguish between what is being said and your own assumptions and emotions. This can be difficult, but you need to manage your emotions. I've heard it said that we think logically, but we act emotionally. I have found this absolutely true.

Being an Effective Listener

One common mistake people make when they are trying to be a more accomplished listener is that they focus on remembering each and every word. That is nowhere near as important as focusing on understanding the key points that someone is making. Listen as though you were taking notes even if you're not. You should be listening for the main points. That is more effective than trying to remember each word. No one expects you to keep up with every single word. In most cases, remembering a summary of what they said is just as important. Hearing people out is letting people present what they have to say without being interrupted. This simple practice is huge in building trust. Most conversations are an exchange of each person saying what is on their mind, rather than a specific response to what the other person said. Concentrate on what the other person is saying before formulating your own response. Think of it like you are doing an interview. Most folks think faster than they can speak. This can be used as an advantage to take mental notes and find ways to keep your mind engaged. By analyzing what the speaker is saying, you draft your response in ways that help to clarify or elaborate on their main points.

Another way to truly understand the conversation is to verify and summarize what is being said. With complex or emotionally heightened conversations, it's important to listen attentively and verify what the other person is saying. Repeating back to the other person a brief summary of the message as you have heard it is a way to be sure you're both on the same page. Getting better at listening can enhance your own life and help you make a more positive contribution to the lives of others. It's also good to prepare yourself for more in-depth conversations or trainings. If you know ahead of time that you will be listening to a formal presentation, a complex topic, or something unfamiliar, it would be helpful to do a little research ahead of time. By acquainting yourself with the basics, you're more likely to engage in discussion and be able to keep up with detailed information.

Acting on what you've learned - Start Small

After attending a training session or conference, the key is to act on the information you picked up. In my experience, the key is to start small. Below is an exercise that will help keep you on track.

Step 1: Place the most impactful information order of priority for conquering or accomplishing them.

Step 2: Take them on one (1) at a time.

Step 3: Secure follow-up resources, such as books, audio recordings, and worksheets that will give you additional details and motivation to conquer each area.

Step 4: Ask a person who models that trait you want to possess to hold you accountable—a coach or mentor.

Step 5: Add the list to your daily priorities list, and apply activity.

Step 6: Spend Fifteen Minutes Each Day (morning or night) getting focused in order to get control of these areas of improvement.

Step 7: Do a five (5) minute checkup on your items at midday.

Step 8: Take five (5) minutes in the evening to evaluate your progress.

Step 9: Allow sixty (60) days to work on one area before you go to the next one.

Step 10: Celebrate with your coach or mentor as you show continued success.

Takeaways:

- **Learning doesn't stop after your formal education or on-the-job training.**
- **Don't wait on "the company" to provide you with training. Go find out on your own.**
- **The single best investment you make is the one you make in yourself. I commend you for buying this book instead of a six-pack of beer because they both were the same price.**

Sales Statistic: HubSpot Research's survey of salespeople revealed more than half rely on their peers to get tips for improving. 44% looked to their manager, 35% to team training resources, and 24% to media.

Peer-to-peer learning is a great way to pick up on what is working. Just make sure you're also getting input from professionals. Always look to get better at what you do. The great performers in all walks of life put in massive amounts of hours training and learning.

21 Simple Tips that will Take Your Sales to the Moon!

Exercise: What are your favorite books or materials that you can re-read?

Find a list of recommended reading at book.itaintrocketsurgery.net

*Link to research: https://bit.ly/TheRiseofOnlineLearning

21 Simple Tips that will Take Your Sales to the Moon!

Chapter 6 – Habits: We are what we repeatedly do

"On Mondays, I get ready to plan my week. On Tuesdays, I plan my week. On Wednesdays, I revise my plan for the week. On Thursdays, I put my plan for the week into my computer. On Fridays, I think about starting my plan for next week."

21 Simple Tips that will Take Your Sales to the Moon!

"True freedom in life comes back to the habits and routines that we instill in our days. Humans fear uncertainty and when your life is built on intention and design it makes going through the process that much easier. If you want peace of mind and success, it starts with creating great habits and designing a life around accomplishing them."

Drewbie Wilson, VP of Sales at Break Free Academy and bestselling author of "Crushing the Day"

Purpose: In this chapter, we discuss the importance of establishing daily routines and avoiding destructive habits

If you have ever followed Greek philosophy (and I did for a short period of time in my early life), or the wisdom of the Stoics, much of the content surrounds itself on internal struggles. Our greatest enemy to our own success is the voice that is between our ears. In the era of Socrates, Plato, and Aristotle, the focus in Greece was development. Their notion was to develop the person in order to build society. The focus was on the individual, and a growing individual would grow a group, which in turn would grow an organization, which in turn would grow a country.

One of the main goals in self-development, whether it's mental, spiritual, emotional, or physical, is to change the habits of how we have lived our lives up until this point. The habits of our daily lives, more than anything else, will govern our growth. Rewiring your mind for excellence starts with habits.

Aristotle said, *"We are what we repeatedly do. Excellence, then, is not an act, but a habit."*
I am not going to spend this time preaching at you about habits that need to be corrected. I will leave you with some suggestions I have noticed being around high-performers and have implemented them in my own life. But instead of telling you what to do, I will show you a list of what poor-performers do, and you may draw your own conclusions.

10 Habits of the Worst Salesperson that will Plummet Yourself Straight to the Bottom of the Leaderboard

Being the best salesperson in your group or company requires dedication, focus, and hard work. But being the absolute worst is an accomplishment that anyone can achieve. You have been watching the top-dog like a hawk to learn what it takes to be the best, but have you ever looked at the folks on the bottom? There are many lessons to learn by taking a good and long look at the ones bringing up the rear. Every sales team has that one guy or gal who never gets their act together. But just as success requires habits and leaves clues, so does ineptitude. Here are ten tips to become the caboose of your sales team:

1. Having a Bad Attitude

Rudeness and unprofessional behavior are unacceptable under any circumstances. Yet surprisingly, you will meet some salespeople who act plain rude with leads and clients, as well as their coworkers and leadership in the company. This type of behavior gives the prospect the wrong impression about your company. The potential buyer does not get a proper picture of the offer, as they will probably not

21 Simple Tips that will Take Your Sales to the Moon!

even wait for the sales call to end. You will lose many sales like this. Plus, being a shithead to the other salespeople on your team will get you no support in your organization.

Do this instead: There is power in being liked. Be yourself, but as the attractive character. The guy or gal everyone wants to be around.

2. Being Late to Everything

Being on time is not only important to a customer but also important to EVERYONE! No one would be happy if their food delivery is late or the cable guy says he is running two hours behind. That would make you angry! The salespeople represent the first contact customers have with your company. First impressions are not set in stone, but they give a lasting view. Being on time for your appointment is the first chance to make a good impression on the client and increase their confidence in your company.

Do this instead: Use a digital calendar with reminders set up. Integrate this into your email calendar as well.

3. Not Listening to the Customer

In order to present the proper solution to a prospect, you need to listen and observe with great focus so that you pick up on what's most important to your client. Let them tell their story. Within their narrative, you will hear a pain point, also called the "Hot Button." Your solution should be geared toward eliminating that pain. If you do not give the potential customer time to explain the problem there are having, you risk the sale by missing their "hot button."

Do this instead: Listen with intent and pick up on what their true pain points are. What solution will relieve the pain?

4. Not Even Trying to Articulate Yourself

Have you ever heard a recording of your sales process? Would you be willing to put $5 on the line for every "Uh..." that was uttered in your sales call? Every salesperson must know how to articulate themselves clearly and confidently. That starts from the greeting, then qualifies the clients with simple questions. When asked a question by the prospect, your answers should also be clear and concise. If you cannot do this, you come across as uneducated on what you're selling.

Do this instead: Communicate clearly with simple language. Clarity trumps complications every time.

5. Being Rigid and Inflexible

A poor salesperson will force all their clients into the same rigid process each time. Every client has their own style, pace, and tone. A great salesperson should be aware of different personalities and various situations. You must be flexible and able to adapt to different circumstances. It's great to dial in your presentation to be the same content, but the buyers are rarely the same. Each buyer wants to feel special and expects the salesperson to understand his circumstances. Being unable to match your prospect will cost you many sales.

Do this instead: Adapt to each client's pace and understanding.

6. Delivering a Poor Pitch

A great way to blow a deal on an interested buyer is to fumble through your presentation. Better yet, you can diminish nearly all your chances by trying to wing it! The presentation may be (or highly likely to be) the first time a prospect will get the full details about your product. If your product is not shown correctly to the Customer, he is very unlikely to buy. Practice your presentation over and over until it becomes ingrained in your mind. Use product literature, if possible, to keep you on track.

Do this instead: Have your presentation down cold so you can deliver with confidence and not get derailed.

7. Talking Only About Price

Poor salespeople will attempt to justify their price, but the most effective way to earn a client is to build value. It is less likely for a deal to close when the salesperson depends on price to close the sales. The prospective buyer will be quick to take advantage when he sees that the deal depends on the cost of the product. The prospect will drive the price as low as they can. The buyer may even hold off and then not even buy until they get a deep discount. Relying on price alone is just asking to take a heavy cut in profits in order to close sales.

Do this instead: Build value in your product or service by tying a benefit you offer to a pain-point it solves.

8. Not Asking for the Sale

You cannot get what you don't ask for. This is a common fault of the salespeople that make up the bottom, but a lethal one. The part of the sale that separates the professional from the amateurs is the close. Getting them to make a buying decision is a result of all the other parts of your sales process falling in line. Many sales have been lost because the salesperson did not know when to close the sale. A good salesperson is in tune with the prospective buyer and knows instinctively when to move to close the sale. If you did all the other parts of your process correctly, you have earned the right to ask for the business. You cannot wait for the client to say, "I'll take it!" Many times, a simple question is all it takes.

Do this instead: Forget learning 50+ ways to close the sale. Look for a signal that they are digging your product and move them to the next step.

9. Hard Selling and Pressuring the Prospect

A "hard sell" is when salespeople try to push the sale on the prospective Customer. Badgering someone to buy your stuff will just give you a poor market reputation. Pressing a buyer will only make them aggressive, and they will try to get rid of that salesperson as soon as possible. It is a proven fact that people love to buy, but nobody likes to be sold. We are in a modern age with choices like we have never had before. The old tricks of sales are very seldom effective. A powerful presentation and asking for sales at the appropriate time is how business is done in the 2020s.

Do this instead: Make your process as easy as possible, and that will make closing the sale smoother.

10. Never Following Up

You had a great sales call, but they did not buy. If they really wanted your stuff, they would call you back. So, I guess we should never try to talk to them again, right? No! Follow up with the prospect until they tell you not to anymore. I'm not talking about pressuring them. A great salesperson will contact the prospect on a regular basis until they buy or tell him or her to buzz off. Follow-up is especially important, and in reality, it's just good manners. If a salesperson does

21 Simple Tips that will Take Your Sales to the Moon!

not know how to properly and professionally follow up, they will end up losing valuable customers and sales. 80% off all sales are closed after the first meeting.

Do this instead: Follow up via text and/or email can be built into your CRM. Regular follow-ups by phone should be set up as reminders.

Success Habits of High-Performers

Time is the only resource that is non-renewable; therefore, time is our greatest resource. We never seem to have enough of it, and it seems to pass too quickly. It will not reset, we will not get any more of it, and we can't slow it down. What we can do is make the most of the time we have and maximize the opportunities.

Here are some simple steps you can take to get the most out of your day:

Plan Your Day

Put 15-30 minutes at the end of your office time to write out your list for the next day. These can be to-do's but also include goal steps. Assemble the necessary info, like phone numbers and paperwork. That way, you are ready when you hit the desk. The night before, put out your clothes for the next day. If you exercise in the morning, have your workout gear ready. You don't want to be fumbling around to get ready. This is also a mind saver. There are fewer decisions to make at the beginning of the day. Wake up with a purpose.

Prioritize the List

Some of the items may have a time schedule. The others need to be numbered for sequence. Get rid of the crappy ones first. Brian Tracy says, "Eat that frog!" We tend to work on the easy stuff first. I get that. But getting that dirty dog out of the way first gives you a confidence boost and a sense of accomplishment. The day will go smoother afterward. If not, at least it's behind you.

Stick to Your List

Check off the items as you go. Avoid distractions. This is very tough in this day and age. We are living in the age of temptations being so readily available. Whatever we think of is right at our fingertips, and there is an app for everything. You must time block for specific tasks, including email, social media, and even your phone. In my business, I assume that every time I pick up the phone, it's going to be a 30-minute call. Keep that in your mind. If I don't have 30 minutes, then I'm not answering. In my voicemail greeting, I give them a number they can text. Many call-backs are avoided with a text message. If you have a business line that is VOIP, make sure it has text capability.

Plan Personal Time

For this, I mean reading and exercise. Hitting the gym is more effective if it's scheduled, and especially if you are working with a trainer. Then you're on their time, and you won't screw around.

For reading, audiobooks and podcasts are great ways to get information if you struggle with books. It's better than listening to the random radio that plays Metallica ad nauseam. Also, I recently found out that your iPhone will read text on your screen. So a Kindle book is also an audiobook instantly!

Can it be made into a process?

21 Simple Tips that will Take Your Sales to the Moon!

There is a simple filter you can use to determine the necessity of a task. And that is:

Eliminate it

Can I eliminate this altogether without hampering my business?

Automate it

Is there a regular item that can just be made into an electronic process?

Delegate it

Can someone else do this? That someone can be a virtual assistant, or if a large enough task, is it better to staff a position internally?

Do it

If it has to be you, then get it done. Try like the dickens to only touch it once. To be Uncle Frank (the grouchy uncle from "Home Alone") for a moment, that is something that drives me bonkers. I can't stand when I handle an issue, and it comes back or requires more follow-up.

Lastly, Be Honest with Yourself

You can fool all of the people some of the time and some of the people all of the time, but there is no fooling yourself. You must live in the true present. If it ain't working, make the change. The result of a part of life not working, and lying to yourself in thinking that it's working, is the same. Just make the necessary change to get on track. A tough but essential question is: "Is what I'm doing now getting me to where I want to be?" If that answer is "no," then change what you're doing.

Takeaways:

- **Establishing daily habits for personal and business life will make your day much more productive**
- **Setup a priority list and work it.**
- **Protect your personal time, and hold it dear.**

Sales Statistics: Strategy planning was on top of the list of changes for 56% of sales agents, followed by performance analysis and strategy coordination with 55%.

2020 marked one of the most challenging periods in modern history, showing just how vital a strategic approach in sales could be. The biggest changes in sales in 2020 were strategy planning, performance analysis, and strategy coordination. Setting your daily process early will create strong foundations. Even if you have been in a role for a while, you can recreate your daily routine.

Exercise: Write out your daily routine and set up time blocks in a Google Calendar

Find a time block guide and Google Calendar tutorial at: book.itaintrocketsurgery.net

Chapter 7 - Your Body: The Machine

"All I know is, I weighed 148 pounds before my boss sent me to that personal growth seminar!"

21 Simple Tips that will Take Your Sales to the Moon!

"When striving to improve your health and fitness, you don't need all the answers to start. Focus on making the next choice a better choice, and if you do that consistently over time, your desired results will follow."

Marc Zalmanoff, Founder of Marc Z Fitness and bestselling author of "Make Good Choices"

Purpose: In this chapter, we talk about how fitness correlates to performance in the sales force.

Being a high-powered sales professional means you can have a hectic schedule. You may be tempted to cut out lunches in order to have more phone appointments or take more leads. You may be stopping at a fast food place for breakfast and a coffee, then again for lunch. Or you may eat okay, but you are a desk jockey and hardly move any part of your body besides flapping your gums (we sales dogs talk a lot)! If any of these scenarios describe part of your day, then take notes in this section.

The human design is more than just going to the office then coming home. A complete package is addressing our physiology and mentality. In his bestselling book "Pillars of Wellness," Dr. Matt Chalmers introduces a framework for fitness called the Pillars of Wellness. They are:

Psychological – The Mind: Our mental input
Biochemical- - The Body:

Brian McKittrick – It Ain't Rocket Surgery

Biomechanical – The Motion: You need regular daily movement
Spiritual – The Soul: Our connection to the universe

Dr. Chalmers takes a natural approach first to optimizing a full body. What is the point of accumulating a massive fortune, only to be too out of shape to enjoy it? Have fun, and taste life's flavors, but be mindful of all parts of the health equation for a fruitful life.

When I went from managing retail stores to being a full-time insurance broker, I started to gain weight. As a store manager, I rarely would sit down at the store. I was pretty much on my feet, walking and moving 10 hours a day. There was no rest for the wicked awesome (as they would say in Massachusetts)! I was continually about 190 pounds, which is fit for a man at 6 foot 2. But when I transitioned to the health insurance office, I pretty much just sat on my tookus the whole day. The weight started to add over a period of time. At the end of December, I had gotten up to nearly 230 pounds, and my waistline had gone from 32 inches to 38. It hit me when I was watching a football game. At the beginning of the game, they showed a picture of the Dallas Cowboys quarterback Dak Prescott and listed him at 6-2, 230 lbs. That hit me like a bucket of ice water to the face! I was the same height and weight but looked nothing like him. I never pictured myself as a fat guy. In my mind, I was the same hard-hitting and hard-throwing baseballer as I was in high school. It never occurred to me that 20 years out of school, I was going to have a belly. That had to change.

When I made the commitment to change this, I sought some help. That help for me came in the form of a home workout program in an app. That program was written by Marc Zalmanoff of Marc Z. Fitness in Frisco, Texas. The home workout was key to me for two reasons: 1. The Corona Virus had shut down gyms in the spring of 2020, and 2. It gave me no excuse to get started and keep it up. By the end of 2020, I had lost the 40 pounds of fat I gained over my time in insurance. I cannot tell you what a confidence boost I experienced when friends and family noticed the weight falling off. I actually gained 10 pounds of muscle in the few months that followed. Marc and I are now working on getting up to 215 pounds, so I can be in baseball shape. I have no plans to try out for the Texas Rangers, being over 40 years old, but that is the physique I am after.

One of the keys to maintaining a healthy weight and healthy daily lifestyle is to eat properly and stop acting like your mouth is the opening of a garbage disposal for junk food. In business, we can be guilty of being "on the go" most of our day. We might be scheduling appointments and phone calls during our lunch hour or might have to grab a quick bite in the car. In most cases, quick bites are usually not the best food for us. Frying and microwaving foods is the quickest way to make them, and we all know that those are not the healthiest items. I actually hope you know that. If that is something you've never heard, then seek the help of a trainer. So I made a list of 10 food items that are actually good for you and can be prepared relatively quickly.

Ten Sources of Healthy Foods:

1. Whole Grains: Soluble fiber to lower cholesterol
2. Berries: Blueberries, Strawberries, Blackberries, Raspberries
3. Lean Protein: Lean Beef, Chicken, Shrimp
4. Fatty Fish: Tuna, Mackerel, Canned Sardines, Lake Trout, Salmon
5. Nuts: Almonds, Cashews, Peanuts, Walnuts, Pecans, Soy

6. Dark-Green Leafy Vegetables: Kale, Spinach, Swiss Chard, Greens
7. Beans: Red, White, Black, Pinto, Kidney, Chickpea
8. Yellow and Orange Fruits and Vegetables: Carrots, Squash, Sweet Potato, Apricots, Cantaloupes, Papayas
9. Cruciferous Vegetables: Broccoli, Cauliflower, Cabbage, Brussel Sprouts, Kale, Collards
10. Yogurt: Non-Fat live culture, or Greek yogurts

Takeaways from this chapter:

- **Get a workout plan that you can stick with; even walking every morning is a start, Don't let your schedule be an excuse.**
- **I highly recommend seeking the help of a professional.**
- **Have a goal in mind.**
- **Replace quick and junk foods with healthy items. There are plenty of choices that are delicious.**
- **East sensible, and it doesn't have to be a complete overhaul unless you eat like a dumpster fire.**

Sales Statistics: 79% of sales executives say a leading driver of hitting new targets is improving the productivity of existing sales agents.

Productivity starts with stamina and health. If you are winded just moving from your car to your desk, then you're not operating up to your full potential. I have personally experienced the difference being highly in tune for productivity makes to your performance.

Exercise: Take a moment to envision yourself as you would love to look and feel. If that is not now, what steps must you take to achieve your best self?

21 Simple Tips that will Take Your Sales to the Moon!

Find more resources on a healthy body and mind at:
book.itaintrocketsurgery.net

Section 2 – The Sales Environment

Chapter 8 - Goals: Your road map to accomplishment

"If you write down your Top 10 goals 1,000 times a day, you can accomplish anything...if you have any time left over."

Brian McKittrick – It Ain't Rocket Surgery

21 Simple Tips that will Take Your Sales to the Moon!

"Not having goals and targets is like rowing without a rudder; you will do a ton of work but never actually reach a destination!"

Mike Claudio, Founder of WinRate Consulting and bestselling author of "#TooStrong"

Purpose: In this chapter, we outline the proper steps of goal setting

It would be very difficult to hit a target you couldn't see, but here's a question for you: "How can you hit a target you don't even have?"

The idea of setting a goal is to have a specified target of what you want to accomplish, or in some cases, need to achieve. In this chapter, we will discuss the process of setting a goal and the steps in order to work your goals properly to achieve them.

You may be asking yourself, "But what do I set goals on?"

There are infinite possibilities as to what to set a goal on. You may have goals for material items, activities, or accomplishments, but in a general sense, I feel it is paramount to have goals to address these four areas of our lives:

Faith - If you are not religious, that is okay. Having faith grows your gratitude toward life, but if you are not devoted to a particular religion or spirituality, then look for ways to increase your gratitude.

Family and Friends - Your group, or the circle of those you associate with. You may not be able to choose your coworkers, but you can choose how much time you spend with them.

Fitness - Your diet and exercise routine, which also can be called genetics. You don't have to be a gym rat; just get your rear end moving 30 minutes or more per day. Even something as simple as a neighborhood walk will do you good. And don't be a food dumpster. Moderate what you eat to some extent.

Finance - Money isn't everything, but it's up there reasonably close to oxygen. In all seriousness, money will open doors to many other opportunities in life beyond just luxury. The more you earn, also means you have more to give. Your grind is how you make your money.

The Goal Setting Process:

Step 1:
At least once a year, you should make a list of all the things you want to do or complete that year.

It really is a fun exercise. This can be anything you want. Cars, houses, trips, activities, toys, family goals, you name it. Go wild! There are no wrong things to put on your list. This can also be done quarterly and monthly, but I have found that an annual idea list helps to clear our mind of all the things we would like to see in our lives. Quarterly and monthly goals are usually surrounded by our business wants and needs.

21 Simple Tips that will Take Your Sales to the Moon!

Step 2:
Clean up the list.

Scratch off anything from the list that is not really your goal. You can do this by asking yourself, "Why?" If the only reason you have to work on this goal is because someone else assigned it to you, then that is a task, not a goal.

Also, scratch off anything that is a distraction from your main hustle or life's purpose. For example, if you're in real estate, why would you set a goal to get your Series 7 securities license? Unless you are trying to pivot out of selling real estate, you have no need for the license a stock trader uses. On the other hand, if you are in insurance and you want to expand your portfolio by adding variable life insurance and variable annuities, then it would make sense to add your series licenses.

Step 3:
Inspire and motivate your goal

List the benefits of reaching your goal. This will help keep the excitement. When I set a goal to write this book, I listed all the rewards of completing the book. Positive outcomes such as: accolades, speaking gigs, interviews on podcasts, esteem, being able to say I'm a published author... And let's not forget the admiration of many adoring fans (I pictured the launch date, the first stop on my book tour to look something like when the Beatles first landed at JFK airport in 1964). I continually reference the visual of completing my book to remind myself of why I was working so hard to get it done.

Step 4:
What are the challenges?

You will need to identify the roadblocks on your journey. The path to reaching your goal will not be lined with rainbows and butterflies. It will be downright nasty. Prepare yourself by clearly defining the challenges you may face along the way. Going back to my book example, my biggest hurdle was time management. I had to fit writing into what was already a tight schedule. What I did was use the blog posts I was already writing for HardcoreCloser.com and then elaborate the posts into book chapters. I also used a voice recorder to capture ideas and notes while I was out exercising.

Step 5:
What skills or knowledge will be needed?

This is where you might need some additional training or education. If you are going after a new project or expertise, you should seek to become the expert. Do not set the bar so low that just getting it done is good enough. There is a ton of information on the web to pick up the knowledge you need to hit your goal. Do not let this area stop you. Many people will get excited about an idea, then deter themselves when they find out they have to learn something new. I see it all the time.

My company offers licensing training for those individuals who want to get into the fast-paced and high-stakes world of insurance. I don't blame them. Many days I feel like James Bond, but armed with a laptop instead of a submachine gun. But what stops lazy people from getting into the insurance industry is when they find out they are required to get a license. This is a turnoff for many who want to get into stocks and real estate as well. You may need to learn something new, but that's not as hard as it might seem. Find the resources, and it will get easier.

21 Simple Tips that will Take Your Sales to the Moon!

Step 6:
Who do I need to align with?

You may have to work with others to reach your goal. You may need mentorship or assistance. List those folks that will play an important role in your life on your road to accomplishment. These may be friends, family, business associates, managers, or mentors. After you list them, you will communicate to them your goal, if you haven't already.

Step 7:
Write out an action plan

"Failing to plan is planning to fail." – Benjamin Franklin

You gotta have a plan, man or woman! The plan is the roadmap to the end result. It is absolutely essential in order for you to achieve your goal.

When I was a kid, the family took a two-week vacation to Disneyland from Fort Worth, Texas. The reason it took so long was that we planned stops at other sites along the way, such as Carlsbad Caverns and the Grand Canyon. We also stayed at campsites instead of hotels. In order for the trip to go smoothly, we needed to map it out. You can't just get in a car and start driving west from DFW and hope to hit Los Angeles, especially if you are planning on making other stops as well. You have to choose the correct road that connects the two cities. The action plan to hit your goal is exactly the same.

Now that you have established a list of what your goals will be, there is one more format to put them through in order to build out the road map. That process is S.M.A.R.T. You may have heard of this before. S.M.A.R.T. or SMART is an acronym for:

S - Specific
M - Measurable
A - Attainable
R - Relevant
T - Timely

By creating SMART goals, we now put our goals under a microscope. Many people set goals but do not clearly define them enough, so they don't see progress. Or, because the goal had no endpoint, they have not truly put the goal into action. Let's work on an example of an income goal.

You might have heard someone say they want to make more money. That is a goal that lots of people set for themselves. The problem with stating the goal of "make more money" is that there is no clear definition. If a salesperson made $40,000 last year, $42,000 is more money. Did they achieve their goal? Kind of, but I doubt those are numbers that the salesperson that is reading this book would have set out to accomplish.

In order to set a money goal, it needs to be laid out meticulously. Here's how we would set an income goal using the SMART format:

Goal: Earn $120,000 in commission within the next 12 months.

S - Specific: I have a specific amount and income source.

M - Measurable: I can measure my success with a number

A - Attainable: Depending on where you are starting, and as long as what you're selling has a solid comp per sale amount, $120,000 is $10,000 per month in income. That should be an attainable goal in any commission sales job.

21 Simple Tips that will Take Your Sales to the Moon!

R - Relevant: "Anyone who tells you money isn't important, will lie about other things, too." - Zig Ziglar
Money opens doors for freedom. It has been that way since the very beginning. Income has relevance in your daily life.

T - Timely: We put a time stamp on it as within the next 12 months. You can break this down further, which we will in just a moment, to the monthly, weekly, and daily cycle. That's where it gets really fun. When you start accomplishing daily tasks that show your progress to the large goal, then you are building momentum.

Now let's look at a breakdown of a SMART goal into daily activities. We have our income goal of $120,000 in a year or $10,000 per month, but that still doesn't take into account how we actually hit the target.

Think about football. There is no such thing as a touchdown play. There is only a series of plays that, if executed properly, move the ball forward to the goal line. Our income goal is exactly the same. $120,000 is winning the game, and $10,000 per month are the touchdowns. You need to execute the playbook in order to score.

Let's break that down with hypothetical metrics. Get with your sales manager, or do your research to find your real numbers from the process below:

INCOME GOAL STEPS

Step 1 Establish a Monthly Income Goal: $_____

Divide your annual income goal by 12

Step 2 – Average Commission Rate: _____%

What percentage do you make per deal? Ask your sales manager for a goal, or look at your last commission statement.

Step 3 – Monthly Sales Revenue (Premium) Goal: $_____

Divide the income goal by the commission rate

Step 4 – Client Transaction (number of sales) Count Goal: _____

Divide the premium by your average sale. For example, my normal health plan policy value is around $5000 per year.

Step 5 – Set a Close Rate Goal – 1 sale in _____ Presentations

What is your average number of leads to a sale? Once you have lead activity and sales, you will more accurately know how many leads it takes for a sale.

Step 6 – Establish a Monthly Presentation Goal:

Multiply the number of policies needed by the number of leads needed pre-sale.

Step 7 – Number of Working Days in a Week:

You most likely aren't working seven days a week. Set an honest and realistic average of how many days you'll actually be in the office each week. And you also need to take into consideration that day you might have to be out for things like your daughter's dance recital or your dog's emergency hysterectomy.

21 Simple Tips that will Take Your Sales to the Moon!

Step 8 – Presentations per Day: _____

Divide the presentation goal by the weekly working days. The better an agent closes, the fewer presentations are needed for achieving the policy goal.

Example

Step 1: $120,000 Annual Income goal - $10,000 monthly
Step 2: 20% Commission Rate
Step 3: $50,000 Monthly Volume Goal
Step 4: 120 Number of Clients – My example is a $500 monthly premium
Step 5: 1 in 10 Target Close Rate
Step 6: 100 Presentations Needed per Month
Step 7: 20 Working Days in a month
Step 8: 5 Presentations Needed per Day

Now there we have our goal-setting process. Take some time to set goals for yourself, and least in the four categories of: Faith, Family, Fitness, and Finance. Work them through the steps and SMART format. Establish your daily routine, and then track your daily progress. I'll leave you with some tips on daily goal activity.

Speak in a positive vocabulary. For instance, change "I got to…" to "I get to…" Think about that for a minute. If you were to complain to a man in a wheelchair, "I've GOT to go do my daily walk." he'd say, "At least you GET to walk!" See the difference?

Takeaways: Tips for Working Your Goals Daily

• Get organized and have a way to track your progress.
• Choose only a few goals to work each week. Maybe the four key areas, faith-family-fitness-finance, plus another one that is more relevant for that particular time.
• Have daily tracking metrics
• Stick to the plan with discipline. Watch out for exceptions.

Sales Statistics: Top-performing salespeople achieve 125% or more of their revenue goals.

The sales agents on top of the leaderboard outperform the rest of their team members because they operate differently than the others. Having clear goals on what you want to achieve is the first step.

Exercise: Use the goal sheet to outline your financial goals. Then it can be used for any other goal you are looking to achieve.

**Download the goal setting worksheet at:
book.itaintrocketsurgery.net**

Chapter 9 – Focus: Point your mind in the right direction

"I'd like you to lead a seminar on *The Power of Focus*."

21 Simple Tips that will Take Your Sales to the Moon!

"Distractions are killing you. This might seem really overwhelming to hear because life is full of distractions. But you can't give in to them - no matter how many there are - because when you do, those distractions take your power away. When you're not focused, you're not productive. And when you're not productive, you can't win."

Ryan Stewman, CEO of PhoneSites, Speaker, and bestselling author of "G-Code"

Purpose: In this chapter, we analyze the need and power of focus in your personal and professional life

The Enormous Power of Focus

Have you ever felt overwhelmed by all the projects you have in front of you? I'm sure you have. It happens to all of us. But, if you want to significantly grow your business or clientele base, you need to learn to focus your efforts. Many sales professionals don't do this. And this is why so many never get anywhere. It's because they're spreading themselves too thin or going about life operating without a specific target to achieve. They have not clearly defined their goal and are not singularity focused on achieving it. That's just asking for frustration and confusion.

The main difference between a flashlight and a laser is focus. They are both beams of light, but one is focused down to a specific spot. The other covers a broad area. The ability to focus is why a sniper uses a precise rifle versus a shotgun.

There are a lot of ways to make money in sales, but you can't expect to do them all at the same time successfully. We see so many hot markets and opportunities presented to us daily. We would go broke in an instant if we tried to pursue every one of them. You need to have focus. Do not try building your empire by next month. Move gradually and methodically. Organize your goals in steps or projects. Pick a project and get it done, then it's time to move onto the next one.

There are three key benefits to buckling down and focusing:

1. Results will come faster

Trying to do too many projects at once is just asking for failure. Nothing will be completed, or they will all remain stagnant. Focus on one project at a time, step by step. Finish, then implement it. Use the money to reinvest in making it more efficient, and place someone in charge of it that will report to you. Results will come quicker, and you'll be able to scale once it's fully dialed in.

2. It removes confusion

If you're not focused on a goal with a deliberate process, you'll get confused. This is just a fact of being a human, and we're all like that. When something shiny or sexy comes along, we look and lose track of what we're doing. If we don't have the plan to come back to, then we will just chase that new thing. Then the next day, we'll have to take an Uber back from a neighborhood we've never been to, nurse a hangover, and hope you still have enough of a commission check left to make your next rent check. If there are too many projects, too many steps, and too many distractions, we're gonna give up on the whole thing.

21 Simple Tips that will Take Your Sales to the Moon!

We all want to believe that we're capable of multi-tasking or managing a bunch of stuff all at the same time. But in reality, only a select few can do that on their own. Either focus on one project until completion or have a team implement it. This will keep your head clear.

3. It will allow you to grow your business more consistently, which leads to scaling your business

If you're a sales professional with a ton of projects going at once, you're gonna leave some money on the table. You won't take your time to squeeze every last penny out of each project, or you will give a half-hearted effort. You won't fully test or tweak things. You'll build and launch too fast, and you'll miss the details. And details are where money is made. Slow down to dive into the project. Take the time to do it right. Take some time to coddle it to make sure it grows as big as possible.

You will also struggle to build a brand or reputation for being the guy/gal that is the go-to for what you offer. If you offer everything, then no one will recommend you. The "flash in the pan" folks don't build a brand. A great sales pro is a brand of their own. You're building a business, and a well-executed project adds to your business's long-term success.

Final Thoughts on Focus:

There are folks making a killing with affiliate sites. And there are other folks crushing it with info-product sites. Still, others are raking it in with membership sites. There's no end to the opportunities for you to make money, but you can't do everything. You need to choose your direction. Choose one project and focus on getting it done. When you look back after 12 months of methodical and gradual improvement in your business, you'll be blown away by your progress.

Ask yourself:

1. What can I do in order to be more effective at focusing?
2. If you see a distraction, determine if it has the potential to help me reach your goal quicker?
3. What advantages are there to keeping my mind on the mission I've committed to?

The key to focus is to break your goals into small and daily action steps. Accomplishing the small task will keep you on pace for the large achievement. And lucky for you, we have discussed goals in the previous chapter.

Distractions seem most attractive when the going gets tough. When the end is too far away to see, it's easy to get sidetracked and lose focus. If you're not careful, you could take several steps back and then be forced to start building from scratch once more. During the tough times is when it's most important to maintain focus, even when you begin to get weary from the grind. The slightest distraction can make a complete mess of your progress. Sometimes saying no to the good things in life today will give us the chance to say yes to the best things later. Anything that is pulling your attention today is likely to still be around when you achieve your goal. Be patient and pay attention to the mission you set out on. Once you've hit the target, take as much time as you want to relax and give attention to other things, but for now, stay the course. Victories are much more fulfilling when you give everything you have in the pursuit of achieving them.

21 Simple Tips that will Take Your Sales to the Moon!

Takeaways:

- **Focus helps to clarify what needs to be done at any given moment of your sales day.**
- **Focus is our super skill to avoid distractions.**

Sales Statistics: Salespeople spend one-third of their day actually talking to prospects. They spend 21% of their day writing emails, 17% entering data, another 17% prospecting and researching leads, 12% going to internal meetings, and 12% scheduling calls.

With the various tasks a salesperson does daily, it's incredibly important to remain focused on each area at the appropriate time. This is dealing with intentionality.

Exercise: What are your focus areas in the categories of: Faith, Family, Fitness, and Finance?

Obtain the focus sheet at: book.itaintrocketsurgery.net

21 Simple Tips that will Take Your Sales to the Moon!

Chapter 10 – Always: Do what works every time

"Every day at work, I swim with the sharks, run with the wolves and fly with the eagles — but I'm still 30 pounds overweight!?"

21 Simple Tips that will Take Your Sales to the Moon!

"Too many people focus on results...yet results come from a solid, consistent, and reliable process. Falling in love with the process is how to ENSURE you're always leveling up. Remember, today's ceiling is tomorrow's floor for ANYONE who is ALWAYS doing the work."

Kris Whitehead, Founder and CEO of New England Custom Remodeling and bestselling author of "Becoming an Agent of Change"

Purpose: In this chapter, we evaluate the impact of doing what works every time.

We have all heard the term, "Always be closing!"

You've probably heard a sales manager bark at the team, "You should always be closing!" The sales manager probably even played that clip from Glengarry Glenn-Ross where Alec Baldwin yells at the group of scrub salesmen.

But what does that phrase even mean?

When I first heard this phrase at a sales meeting, I took it to mean: everything you do in the sales process should be pointed to the closing stage, and make the close easier by streamlining the sales process so that your client experience has no roadblocks that can prevent the close.

We all know that the close is where the money is, but what about the word "always"? I think that this is the key part of this sales catchphrase.

The word "always" is defined as: at all times; on every occasion. That means every single time. This then gets us to thinking, "Am I taking the necessary steps to closing prospects? Am I doing what works to make closing easier?

How often are you executing each building block of the sales process?

Most of the time?

9 out of 10 times?

99 out of 100 times?

99.9% of the time?

In coaching and training salespeople, I commonly hear them say that they will do what they know to do most of the time or even go as far as to tell me they do this 99.9% of the time. But why skip any of the steps in the sales process? We have no way of knowing if a prospect would have bought if we are not executing every sales building block. The average person will accept "99.9% of the time" as good enough. How accurate is 99.9% anyway? 99.9% is only missing 1 of 1000. Would you be happy with the following results of 99.9%?

At a 99.9% accuracy every year in America:

1,800 patients will have their cancer misdiagnosed

3,853 babies will be given to the wrong parents

21 Simple Tips that will Take Your Sales to the Moon!

10,980 cars will hit the roads without being safety tested

253,000 tax returns will be incorrectly filed

142.6 million letters will be misdelivered

Six million cell phone calls will be misconnected – PER DAY!

These results of 99.9% would be tragic and unacceptable. You cannot skip pieces of your sales process and think that you are fulfilling your responsibility as a sales professional. You are shortcutting the client and being ineffective. I once heard someone say, "Don't half-ass anything! If you are going to do something, use your whole ass." And that's exactly right.

Think about professional athletes. They spend hours on end practicing and redefining their mechanics. The reason for this is that during a game, they want their instincts to take over and cut down on thinking during play. In order to do this, they meticulously practice each step until it's so ingrained in their psyche that they are able to operate just from memory and instinct.

You can find fantastic examples of always taking the steps and refining your form by watching hall of fame athletes. One of the best showcases of always is one of my favorite athletes, Dirk Nowitzki of the Dallas Mavericks. Dirk was one of the league's best shooters in history and was an anomaly being a 7-footer who shot around 88% for his career at the free-throw line. The phenomenal thing about Dirk was that his form was incredibly consistent. He literally used the same motion for his free throws every single time. Dirk once set an NBA record hitting 21 straight free throws in a 2011 playoff game. They also won the championship that year.

Your sales process needs to be scripted to the point of being mechanical.

By having a mechanized process, you eliminate the variables and can pinpoint exactly where a breakdown happened. If you were having car trouble, the mechanic would work through a checklist to try and find the problem in the mechanical sequence. Your sales process should be the same. I use the same questionnaire in the same sequence to qualify prospects, and I do it every single time. This keeps me on track throughout the sales and keeps my client service level high.

By executing all the proper steps of the sales process, you can eliminate reasons your client isn't buying or help you to pinpoint why they do not move forward with the sale. Taking the proper steps in your sales process will eliminate potential roadblocks and make the sale easier to close.

Takeaways:

- **If you have something that's working for you, continue to do it.**
- **Refine your process until it can be replicated every time, without fail.**
- **Look to operate like a sales machine, without sounding mechanical.**

Sales Statistic: Nearly six in 10 salespeople say that when they figure out what works for them, they don't change it.

Passion ties right into this. Once you find areas in your role that you love to do, perfect them, and then maximize their effectiveness by being the best you can at them.

21 Simple Tips that will Take Your Sales to the Moon!

Exercise: What is working in your sales process, but you need to execute consistently?

**Grab a copy of the worksheet on Always at:
book.itaintrocketsurgery.net**

21 Simple Tips that will Take Your Sales to the Moon!

Chapter 11 – Innovation: Creating selling systems

"I've been promoted to Executive Director of Sticky Note Management and Distribution."

21 Simple Tips that will Take Your Sales to the Moon!

"Thinking outside of the box is a prerequisite to innovation, not the solution. To truly innovate, you must take massive action against those thoughts and combine it with passion and purpose."

James Golden III, Founder and CEO of PMG Pavement Management Group and bestselling coauthor of "Million Dollar Dads"

Purpose: In this chapter, we look at ways to innovate within our sales fields.

Innovation

I feel that, as a whole, sales professionals really need to examine how well we are handling the point of customer contact. Are the recent innovations that are removing salespeople from the transactions the result of innovations to make sales easier, or the consequence of poor sales performance, which is leading to clients repeatedly bypassing the salesperson?

Lee Iacocca, former Chairman of Chrysler Corporation (perhaps at that date the world's Number 1 salesperson), said:

"The future of the automobile industry will be decided upon at the point of contact."

Let's reflect for a minute on that statement. What changes in your industry have been made that address the point of consumer contact?

If anything, aren't we taking away the human element in many of our sales processes?

Self-Checkout at the grocery store.
Ordering your own food at a fast-food restaurant.
Ordering online.
Ordering a car with Carvana.
Buying insurance completely online with no interaction with an agent.
Getting food delivered to you.

And now, after many more COVID regulations are forcing contactless interactions, consumers will be put in more sales transactions where the salesperson is removed or at least given a smaller role. Over time the sales industry will put less importance on the reliance on personal touch in sales and business. One thing to explore in this growing trend is this question:

Is the elimination of human interaction in sales caused by automation and convenience, or is it because the vast majority of salespeople have done a poor job?

Take an intense look at your industry. Are you forcing consumers to buy the way you want them to, or have you made any adjustments to how the prospect is shopping?

I know in my industry, insurance, most of the carriers have not caught onto the simplicity of clients finding information and premium pricing online, or even the best practice of electronic enrollment. And insurance agents are not helping. They force customers to call them, and that call must take

21 Simple Tips that will Take Your Sales to the Moon!

place during standard business hours. The prospect wants to start shopping online, but very few agency offices have a strong website. Even if they did have a working website, it would give very little information. They all have forms or buttons for a "FREE QUOTE," but that quote is over the phone. The buyer is back to making a phone call at a time convenient for the agent. That's a call they dread making because they know it will be a pain in the ass.

I heard about a study that prospects are willing to pay just slightly extra for life insurance so that they don't have to talk with an agent. When I heard that, my heart cracked a little. Have we become that bad to deal with?

The way to combat all of this is to make your buying process simpler. You need to have the functionality to live where the prospect is comfortable. Even if your business has certain requirements or regulations, you still need to start the conversation wherever the buyer is before you start forcing them into your rules.

Are you set up to capture a lead and start the sales process:

On your website?
From an email?
In Facebook?
In Linked-In?
On You-Tube?
On Instagram?
From a social media direct message?
From a phone call, if you are an in-person salesperson like cars, retail, or real estate?

The point is to live where the prospect starts, then transition to the required avenue for your sales process.

It's important for leads to be able to find you anywhere, but just as important is to be able to offer information online and begin the sales conversation in that same sphere. You must be able to move the sales conversation forward from that initial contact. But the key to getting sales from digital contacts is that you only need to sell the next step. The first thing you need to do is to find out if the contact wants to stay in the same space or move offline. When I first get a contact, my response will go something like this:

"Hello, Brian. I was referred to you for a health insurance plan."

"Thank you (name) for reaching out. I'd be happy to assist. Would you prefer to look at information online or have a brief phone call?"

What I've done is give them a choice, and I only moved the sale to the next step. I didn't go into a pitch or start trying to qualify them into a plan, or even worse, try to close them on a deal.

Innovation doesn't have to mean that you are breaking new ground with an invention or a new product that solves the world's problems. Innovation in sales is looking for new ways to make the client experience: easier, of higher quality, to provide better service, less expensive, a better value, and any number of ways to elevate your sales process for your prospects. There are any number of ways to make an improvement in your industry or do something your competitors do not.

The Power of Social Media

It's no secret the world is on social media. Facebook currently has over 2 billion daily users. YouTube has almost

21 Simple Tips that will Take Your Sales to the Moon!

2 billion users. Instagram has 1 billion. Twitter has approximately 330 million, LinkedIn has 303 million, and Pinterest has 250 million. Your prospects and customers are using at least one, if not multiple social media platforms. With such a large number of people using social media every single day, it's probably the most powerful way to grow your business. Social media platforms have shrunken the world and will allow you to attract new customers or connect with audiences that might not have ever found you. If your business isn't dependent on a physical location, then you're now expanding your customer reach through social media. By being strong on social media, you can also establish yourself as a leader in your industry, even if what you're saying is not groundbreaking; just by being online saying it publicly can instantly establish a celebrity type of expertise.

Optimize Your Social Media Profile

Make your profile page attractive and informative. You want your profile to be inviting. Most users go to social media to be engaging. Here are some suggestions to optimize your profile(s):

Use a professional username. This should be your full name and might mention your company.

Use a high-quality profile photo. The photo does not have to be done by a professional photographer, but it should be clean and with a good resolution. Use an actual picture of yourself, NOT a logo. Your logo can be somewhere else.

Upload a professional cover photo. Nearly all social media platforms allow you a cover photo. This is the photo that spans the top of your social media profile and sits behind your profile photo. This also should be high-quality and as professional as possible.

Write a compelling biography section. This is the section where you tell a brief story of yourself and tell the audience a little about your business. You want to be compelling and concise. List what you do, what problem you solve, and who you want to work with. What is it that you do that sets you apart from everyone else?

Complete all your contact information. If you're trying to grow your business using social media, you want to make it as easy as possible for prospects to contact you. Include your main business information and as many possible ways to contact you as possible.

Think about how it is you want to represent yourself and your business online. Your social media page may be the first point of contact for some potential clients, so it's important that your profile feel professional.

Start Following the Right People in Your Industry

Find ways to follow influencers in your industry. For example, if you're a financial adviser, follow other financial advisers in your industry. If you're in the car business, follow influential people in the car industry. Once you've started following leaders in your field, interact with the material they share. Make comments or share them on your own page. You're looking to develop relationships and simply be part of the conversation. You also want to join groups on Facebook and LinkedIn that are related to your industry. There are groups on literally every professional industry around. After joining a group, the focus is to add value, not promote yourself. As you follow others in your industry and participate in groups, be mindful of the kind of information that is being shared. What posts are resonating? This is the type of content that you want to be sharing with your audience, BUT only if you can share in YOUR voice.

21 Simple Tips that will Take Your Sales to the Moon!

Also, consider following blogs and websites like Quora that let any user post a question, and then other users try to answer that question.

Engage With Your Audience (Social Media Friends/Followers)

The power of social media is creating conversations between you and your audience. Conversations are the key to getting more clients through social media. It is important to consistently engage with your followers to build relationships. You gain clients through social media by having conversations that solve problems, not just posting content. Have this engagement with authenticity (aka "Keep it Real"). This will attract new followers, which can, in turn, become clients. Engagement boosts social media posts. The posts with the most reactions, comments, shares, and overall activity get shown more than posts with very little action.

What are some ways that you can create conversations with your followers?

• Ask questions or make statements that will encourage discussion (decide your comfort level of controversy).
• Do live videos in which you talk directly with your audience.
• Conduct polls or ask for comments on a particular subject.

We will look at social media again in the chapter on prospecting.

Ways to Find Innovation

Studying History

Our world changes so fast now; we need to stay on the cutting edge. Creativity has served mankind well over the years, and it's very interesting to study the past but also inspirational. It may change over time, but in my experience, creativity moves slowly at first until it can no longer be ignored. Success stories from historical figures can be an inspiration. Many of the greatest achievements have come from historical figures. Looking at the bold steps, they took on their journey can be a typecast for your business. Sometimes the innovations hit big right away, but in other ways, it was more gradual, but keeping the focus and perseverance in their creativity allowed them to change the world. Studying pioneers such as Benjamin Franklin, Thomas Jefferson, George Washington-Carver, Henry Ford, the Wright Brothers, Steve Jobs, Elon Musk, and many others who pushed the envelope of what the world thought can provide a massive amount of inspiration in the way you view your business. By reading and understanding their beginnings, inspirations, challenges, and turning points, you may resonate with some similarities between you and one of them. And don't think for a second that your role is too small. Innovation comes at all levels. For goodness sake, the walkie-talkie was invented by an army infantryman, not a general.

Inventions that didn't catch on at first.

When you hear the phrase, "Think outside the box!" sometimes the box may be the time and era that something new was created. There have been some great inventors who introduced concepts before the world was even ready for them. Don't let that deter you from sharing any ideas that pop up for you. You may have notes in a journal that you feel are too silly to share with the world. Remember that

21 Simple Tips that will Take Your Sales to the Moon!

once your innovation is fascinating enough, it can appeal to others. It can convince them that it's actually something they want.

Almost every movie is about overcoming massive obstacles, or there is a difficult challenge to figure out. Through hard work and continuing to push through, they defy all odds and succeed. Unlike the movies that always have them finding clear skies at the end of the road, there must be a perpetual push to keep developing your craft and business. These stories provide a wonderful glimpse into what is possible. Personally, I have always been more intrigued by documentaries and films based on a true story. I mainly like watching something I can learn from. Fiction is nice, but truth is much stranger, and you may have your mind opened to a world of possibilities. If they can do it, so can you!

As I watch a real-life story, I ask myself:

How do they keep moving forward?
Are there special strategies they employ?
How were they able to overcome the roadblocks?

If you see examples of when things seemed impossible, then observe the people who created a new path; you will open your eyes as one more person to change the face of the future. Then you should realize that a bump in the road doesn't push you back but really only slows you down or merely diverts you somehow; you will keep moving forward. Keep in mind, pilots don't turn around from their journey just because some bad weather comes up. They simply fly higher. If you really want what it is you're after, then bumps in the road won't take you off course. The drive to achievement creates a spirit of fearlessness and boldness. That's what's needed to innovate in your market.

Find out what customers in the marketplace are saying, study the success stories of the greats and those that overcame adversity, and you will open your mind to new paths of sales that your competitors are not taking advantage of. These sources can provide the inspiration you need to be creative. Take a different approach. That's a surefire way to stand out from everyone else. You can expect great results when you elevate the thought process for innovation.

Don't worry about the opinion of the "little world." The "little world" or "little folks" are the general public naysayers who have a tendency to be short-sighted, cautious, and with a limiting belief of opportunity.

It is very easy to get discouraged by the lack of support from "little folks." Keep in mind, most people go to their grave with the passion still within them. Don't fret for a moment that your ideas and projects are not exciting those in your inner circle. They are most likely not your audience.

If you want to write a book, but your immediate friends and family shit on it, ask them, "How many books have you written?" If the answer to the question is anything less than, "I was a bestseller," then their view might not have any meaning. The world is looking for your contribution to society. It may make you sad, but your clients are the public, not friends and family. Chances are, they aren't accomplishing anything.

This will make you feel better. Here are a few examples of classic short-sightedness:

In 1878 British Parliament called Thomas Edison's light bulb "a fairy tale."

21 Simple Tips that will Take Your Sales to the Moon!

In 1927 H.M. Warner, co-founder of Warner Brothers said, "Who the hell wants to hear actors talk?"

In 1995 Clifford Stoll of Newsweek said, "The truth is no online database will replace your daily newspaper."

Takeaways:

- **Look for ways to improve the client experience.**
- **The consumer public rewards new ideas and processes.**
- **Don't fret over the opinions of critics.**

Sales Statistics: 65% of salespeople who use social selling fill their pipeline, compared to 47% of reps who do not.

Social media is another example of using technology to maximize your business. It's an example of using innovation in prospecting. Those that are taking advantage are being rewarded.

Exercise: Look at the areas of your organization where you feel are archaic. How can they be improved?

**Find a guide on sales systems at:
book.itaintrocketsurgery.net**

Chapter 12 – Niches: Who is your target customer?

"Business is lousy. Maybe I should have done more market research first."

21 Simple Tips that will Take Your Sales to the Moon!

"When you niche down, it becomes a gold mine of understanding and positioning yourself as the only one who truly understands your prospects unfilled dreams and desires."

John Highley, Founder of Tactical Dent Tools and bestselling author of "The Marketing Savage"

Purpose: In this chapter, we examine the proper way to define our ideal client and market niche

Are you marketing to a wide audience or to a specified niche?

When you are defining your marketing strategy, you will need to decide whether you will be a one-stop-shop for your industry or if you will carve out a specific piece of the market, called a niche, for which you will establish yourself as the specialist. Either is fine. It is a question to ask yourself, and only you can properly answer it. There is no wrong answer here. You just need to have that answer.

A niche is defined as: a specialized segment of the market for a particular kind of product or service.

In other words, a niche is a group of people with common interests and/or the same hobbies. The group could have the same social background and/or ethnicity. The niche could be a subset of another demographic. Each category of a niche will have the same desires and needs and will need information and a solution to their problems. Your niche may be an extremely targeted market, or you can drill down into the specifics of a niche to further define your market.

Defining a Niche: Here are some steps to take:

Be Unique

If there is nothing that differentiates you from your competition, you become common. Webster defines the word common as "ordinary or not special," and the only way buyers select one common service over another is price.

Take inventory of your skills, experience, and knowledge. Are you a specialist in some area? Are you an expert in certain facets of your business? These and other differentiators can make you unique and valuable to a select group of clients.

Define Your Ideal Client, then Choose Prospects Carefully

After you've decided whether to offer a wide range of products and services for your industry or if you'd rather be deep on just one type, the next step is to define the ideal client.

Every business has an ideal target customer, and it is important to know who that customer is, what that customer looks like, and how they act. The details about your ideal customer will influence almost every decision made in your business, from marketing channels and email copy to your imagery, logo design, and even the professional attire of the company staff.

21 Simple Tips that will Take Your Sales to the Moon!

Your ideal client is someone who meets a series of criteria that you determine from dissecting your current customer base or network. We can look at the standard demographics such as age, gender, height, and weight, but that is not well defined enough to say they are your perfect or ideal customer to do business with. Look for ways to more clearly define the customer that you are targeting. Look for a deeper understanding with attributes like where they live, their hobbies and interests, what they eat, where they went to school, brands they wear, and especially what they like and follow on social media. You must also make a list of what their pain points and problems are, so the solution you provide is tailored to their specific needs.

At the beginning of your sales career, you may have to work with any client that you can. That is okay. As you build your clientele, you need to start to attract your ideal customer. This is called an "avatar." The word "avatar" refers to an icon or manifestation made to represent a person or character. Just like the avatar you make for a video game or your social media account, this is a construction of the qualities you want to see in your ideal customer.

To begin taking control of the way you are attracting the clients for your business, write down the attributes of the people you want as clients and then go out and get them with targeted marketing. I hope the first item on your list of attributes is that they are people you enjoy spending time with. Being a business owner is far too difficult to work with people you don't like just to earn a living.

Turn away people who don't meet your criteria. When you reject or refer away potential clients that don't fit your customer avatar, it tells the world that you don't just work with anyone; you are selective, which raises your perceived value. It also makes you unique from other businesses that will work with anyone who can bring them a paycheck.

Research Your Niche

Before you spend all your time defining a niche, and working on a website and writing up eBooks, you will need to make sure that your potential customers are going to be interested in what you are selling.

Examine your product or service:

What do you want to sell?
What is an area that you have specialized knowledge about?
What is your passion?

Selling an informational or transactional product online is easier than selling a service, but selling a service online makes more money with monthly memberships.

There are three reasons why a customer will want to buy your product:

- Your product or service solves a problem for your customer
- Your product or service makes life easier or more comfortable for your customer.
- You are very passionate about your product or service, and it shows in everything you do.

Do your homework now, and find what people want.

- Do your current clients frequently ask for a product or service that you do not offer?
- Is there a natural add-on to what you sell that you currently do not offer?

21 Simple Tips that will Take Your Sales to the Moon!

Answer these questions in your market research. Also, see how many competitors you have. The fewer, the better, but look at their gaps, and fill that need in your market. This is your chance to widen your net and catch more clients. The answer to this question may come from your ideal client themselves, or from what your competition is doing, or even more powerful, what they are NOT doing.

Once you find your avenue and passion, ask yourself how this serves your customers.

You want to provide an excellent service to each and every person that spends their money with you. This cuts down on complaints, bad reputations, and, worst of all, chargebacks.

There needs to be a selection process of how we choose who we want to work with as clients. There are many benefits of a clearly defined customer base:

1. You're able to add more value, which strengthens our client relationship
2. You can focus your marketing strategies
3. You can innovate in a clear direction and focus
4. You can reduce wasted time and effort

Process for defining the ideal customer:

"Choose your client, choose your life."
Seth Godin, Marketing Instructor and 20x bestselling author of titles such as "Purple Cow" and "Tribes."

You first need to know who ISN'T your customer. Chasing every sale will cause frustration, and being a generalist is not as powerful as being a specialist.

Identifying your customer includes clearly defining who they are, their interests, and what they do. The list below is a starting point for common client descriptors. Depending on what you do, you may have more specific traits, but this will serve as a basis to get started.

Answer the questions in this list, as well as any specifics to the needs of the buyers of your product or service. Once you identify these qualities, then this is the model for the connections you make in networking and who you seek in prospecting.

Common Traits to Build the Description of Your Dream Client:

Gender: Male / Female

Age range

Marital Status: Single – Married – Divorced – Widowed – Single-Parents

Do they have children?

What is their physical location?

Occupation: What do they do for a living?

Financial status: What is their income range?

Education: High School – College Degree – Master's Degree – Military Service

Health: Are they taking care of themselves? Do they share a common medical condition?

21 Simple Tips that will Take Your Sales to the Moon!

Habits: Do they share a common habit or routine?

Hobbies: What do they do in their spare time?

Interests: What would they LIKE to be doing in their spare time?

Religious: Is there a common religious view?

Political Interest: Do your customer have a political tendency that influences them?

What are they consuming on the internet?

Websites they visit

Videos they watch on YouTube

Search phrases

Industry slang and jargon they research

Who are their influencers?

Where on social media are they most active?

What time of day are they on social media?

What books or magazines (printed or electronic) are they reading?

What does your dream client really want?

What are your client's biggest struggles or problems?

Who are the competitors of your business they might be looking at?

As you construct your client description, keep the format below in mind. This will be how you design your prospecting plan (next chapter) and opening statement (like an elevator pitch) to explain to them who you are and what you do. I am going to use an example from health insurance sales, but ANY industry will be able to insert the applicable statements for what you sell.

Problems – What problems are your ideal clients facing?
- Where to find a health plan outside of group coverage or the ACA marketplace
- There are so many health insurance carriers
- Most customers have an agent for every plan they use
- Every time the client's shop, it's such a pain
- Many families are not financially sound
- Many companies are not financially strong enough to go 60-90 days at a loss of revenue (look at how many companies went belly up in 2020)

Questions – What questions do your clients need answered?
- "ACA is too expensive; where else can I go?"
- "There are so many plans; which is best for me?"
- "My family needs to be financially protected, but how?"
- "What am I missing I haven't heard of?"
- "(Small Business Owner) Where do I start?"
- "Where do I find an agent that will do it right?"
- "Why haven't I heard of these plans (plans outside of the ACA Marketplace)."

21 Simple Tips that will Take Your Sales to the Moon!

Roadblocks – What is preventing them from finding what they want?
- Costs
- Looking for an alternative to the high-cost big carriers
- Few choices available
- Knowledge: They don't know that they don't know

Results – What is the result your client is looking to achieve?
- Be properly covered
- Be within their budget
- Want a quality plan they can use when they need to
- Peace of mind knowing they have protection

Title – What are you calling yourself?
- Insurance and Finance Specialist (advisor | expert)

Mission Statement – What is your personal message so your clients know your mission?
- To be the trusted advisor(s) for small businesses and self-employed persons to find the insurance protection and finance capital they need in a simple and efficient manner.

Ideal Client – In a few sentences, summarize your ideal client
- Self-Employed or small business owner that sees insurance as important for themselves and employees.
- Financially stable, above-average income.
- Educated in money and its value.
- Specifically, target real-estate, and now talking to fitness professionals.

Hangout – Where are they visiting online (from the exercise)?

Elevator Pitch – Your quick statement of who you are and what you do?
- We are an insurance brokerage offering the complete set of plans you would need and want for your business and family—all your plans with one agent and agency.

Superpower – What do you do better than anyone else?
- Matching the proper plan to the client's needs in a simple and efficient manner.

Challenge – What is your obstacle to overcome in attracting clients?
- My challenge is to be known for helping with all types of insurance and have them think of me when a plan need arises.

Takeaways:

- **There are riches in the niches. Find your small gold mine. Clearly define your ideal client description to know who to target in prospecting.**
- **Speak to their problems and challenges, then how you can assist with their situation.**

Sales Statistic: More than 40% of prospectors don't target the right audience.

One of the biggest mistakes in sales is pursuing the wrong target audience. Losing time with people who won't make a purchase is a significant issue for 41% of prospectors. While a perfect fit is not always going to happen for any product category, doing some background work before going after

21 Simple Tips that will Take Your Sales to the Moon!

prospects can help improve sales. The first step is to clearly define the market and customer base, then create your social media and other marketing strategies.

Exercise: Define in minute detail your perfect client

**We have a Perfect Client Worksheet at:
book.itaintrocketsurgery.net**

21 Simple Tips that will Take Your Sales to the Moon!

Chapter 13 – Prospecting: Where are today's buyers?

"I think my spell-checker is broken. It keeps changing l-u-c-k to p-r-e-p-a-r-a-t-i-o-n."

21 Simple Tips that will Take Your Sales to the Moon!

"No matter what you're selling, when you have the right strategy, ask the right questions, and deliver valuable content, you will get the best leads of your life IF you follow the correct steps."

Vince Reed, Founder of SetupMyAds.com and bestselling author of "Internet Traffic and Leads"

Purpose: In this chapter, we brainstorm on where we find our ideal clients

Prospecting in the 21st Century is all about finding where your ideal clients are and how they want to shop your product or service. This includes the websites they visit, the social media sites they most use, and what contact lists they will appear on. For the most part, prospecting efforts don't generate a rapid return. Your goal must be to increase your chances of successful prospecting in the long term. To do so, make a prospecting plan that engages in multiple areas.

Association Lists

Many times, our ideal client is a member of an organization that has a professional license (real estate, insurance, doctors, attorneys, etc.) or an alumni association. In many states, a licensee list is available for free from the state's license department, depending on the category. Even if your state does not offer this for free, it is usually a small fee. The list is names and addresses; many will include phone numbers and emails.

Information Lists

You can acquire pinpointed lists by shopping databases. Depending on your industry focus, there is a website dedicated to the information you're looking for; whether it's business or consumers focused. You can slice the data in as many ways as you like or be as deep as you want. See the website link at the end of the chapter.*

Mailers

Purchased lists almost always come with addresses. Mailers are still very much a strong marketing resource. The highest bang for your buck these days are postcards. A quality color graphic postcard has a unique advantage in that there is no envelope, so it almost always gets read. I like to have a call to action, then use a QR code to have them visit a weblink. That way, you're getting back into the digital space.

Cold Email

Do not think for a second that email is dead. SPAM emails are dead, but targeted emails that hit the contact's inbox are highly effective. Marketing to your ideal client with an offer that speaks to their needs is still a great way to add regular fresh leads to your database. The key here is to make it to their inboxes. To increase your odds of getting in front of your names, obtain a list of fresh data (paid lists are higher quality), scrub the data for email address verification, have your account information records set up properly, and send emails at a quantity per day that is sufficient, but not overwhelming, or you may get you flagged as a SPAMMER.

21 Simple Tips that will Take Your Sales to the Moon!

SMS Text

Text marketing is similar to email marketing but boasts an open rate of over 90%! However, be careful. In almost all cases, to send a text message, the lead must need to opt-in. So that means if you are going to send mass amounts of texts, purchased leads are the sources to use. The most cost-effective will be aged leads. Some lead companies offer 30-60 day old lists of leads that cost under $1 per name.

DISCLAIMER: Double check your state rules, but in most cases, a lead cannot be called or sent a text message after being 90 days old.

Social Media Posts

The Problems that Social Media Prospecting Solves:

- Running out of warm leads
- Not having enough conversations
- Not enough organic traffic
- Doing too much convincing clients to do business with you
- Prospects have stopped reaching out to you

Choose Your Platform(s)

In the beginning, instead of trying to post on every social media platform, focus on the one or two that will have the most impact on your business. A simple trick is to post from Instagram and link your Facebook. You will hit 2 in 1. LinkedIn tends to be more business-based. Choose according to your potential client flavor.

To find your most effective site, you need to know your ideal client:

Where do they spend their social media time?
Where do they like to interact with brands and businesses?
What sites have an influence on them to purchase?
What platforms do the biggest influencers in your industry use?

Publish most of your content on the social media site where your audience hangs out the most to get the most interaction and conversations. If you do not know where your audience spends most of their social media time, look at the content you've already posted on social media and see what has gotten the biggest response. Also, consider when choosing your social media platform is what you are selling. One platform may be more effective than another for the products or services you sell. Start small in the beginning and get one site down first before moving onto the next. You do not want to spread yourself too thin across multiple social media platforms. You will do far better results by hitting the main platform instead of spreading yourself thin posting on multiple websites.

What matters most is not the platform you choose, but rather that you choose one and stick with it. Consistency is the most effective way to win an audience when it comes to social media.

Social Media Posting

Choose the frequency at which you will be posting. Once you start, you must post at least daily to keep up consistency, but optimally, you should post 2-3 times per day, depending on the times of day your ideal client is on social media. For small business owners and entrepreneurs, they usually visit Facebook in the early morning, and then again in the evening, or late night. LinkedIn is actually used throughout the day for those that are actively networking. Instagram can be used pretty much anytime, in my experience.

Once you've created a posting schedule, begin posting consistently content that will add value to your audience. In creating an audience for business or prospecting, you're not just posting randomness just to post. Instead, you're trying to provide your audience with high-value information. Your content should be helpful in some way to your audience.

Content should create a response of some type. Get your audience to:

- Think about a topic differently
- Take a new action
- Smile, or Laugh
- Learn something new

Valuable posts include:

- Inspirational quotes
- Tips and tactics
- Tutorial videos
- Live videos
- Interesting pictures

You don't always have to be a motivational speaker type. Sometimes all you need to do is entertain. But do it in a way that speaks to your audience. Whenever you post on social media, ask yourself the following question: Will this be adding value to my audience? If it is not something of value or entertainment that is in your voice and your audience would enjoy, then don't post. Be very careful of controversy. Be yourself, but unless you want to build a brand around edginess, it won't add much value. And should that be your angle, you will start to attract many followers you would not want to do business with. It's better to base your style on positivity and fun.

If you're not sure which types of content add the most value to your audience, try experimenting with different formats. You might find that videos perform better than photos or that your audience really likes tutorials and tips.

You may be thinking, I don't have time to constantly be posting! Using a tool like Buffer or Hootsuite, you can actually schedule weeks, or even months, of posts in advance.

Use of Hashtags

Hashtags are words or phrases with the "#" symbol added to the beginning. For example, #DadJokes, #ItAintRocketSurgery, or #CartoonBrian.

Hashtags are used to group posts by subject. Using a hashtag will group your post with others about the same subject. These are very useful in growing your audience on Instagram or Twitter. Users in these platforms will search posts by hashtag topics, and you can gain followers that enjoy those posts.

To add hashtags, at the end of your post, just type a "#" symbol before the topic words, and the platform will begin to populate that word. The word will be highlighted and then linked to those other posts. The power of hashtags is that they allow you to get your content in front of a broader audience. If done correctly, your post can be seen by thousands, even millions, of people.

Experiment with your posts

21 Simple Tips that will Take Your Sales to the Moon!

To truly succeed in prospecting on social media, you'll need to experiment a little to find your style and see what works the best. Mix up the content because different types will resonate with your audience. It's also helpful to have a theme by day, or times of day. One common theme of "Motivational Monday" is a big one in the entrepreneur space. You can either follow that trend for your audience or do the opposite. For your style, or your ideal clients, video may work well, while inspirational posts fall flat. You just have to test them out. Once you have discovered what adds the most value for your audience, post more of this content so that you generate the most engagement. This will become a massive cycle to connect with more people on social media.

What do you do when you are in a cold spell of leads?

Have you ever experienced a downtime in your leads? This is bound to happen occasionally. Pro-active sales professionals will aggressively create their own traffic. Relying solely on inbound leads will earn you the team award for "Caboose of the Sales Train."

Here are some prospecting areas that, when done correctly and regularly, will give you a steady flow of strong leads:

Focus on Your Own Clientele Base

When manufacturers create customer service index surveys, the intent was to monitor customer satisfaction. This causes many salespeople to conduct their presentations and sales calls, delivery, and follow-up to boosting their customer service score. In actuality, the goal should be to create a perfectly satisfied customer. By focusing on your current customer base, this is key to repeat business. When you are in your sales call, you should not be attempting to sell your product today, you should be attempting to sell your prospect the next five times. The attempt to be their life-long salesperson requires contacting your customer at regular intervals and sending routine contacts such as a monthly newsletter (email or mail) or holiday email to keep yourself in their memory. A great example of regular positive contact is to send out birthday notices by email or by card. If you can maintain satisfied customers, you will see repeat business. In your regular contacts, remind your client of the other offers you have that they may be interested in.

Seek and Cultivate Referrals

Every salesperson should be asking for referrals at the end of the initial sales call. A prospect happy enough to buy should be happy enough to send their friends and family. Another key is to cultivate referral sources to maximize the flow of organic prospects. Build strong relationships to solicit referrals from: customer base, social groups like BNI or your city's Chamber of Commerce, churches, schools, friends and family, and social media groups. Many insurance agents, CPAs, financial advisors, and bankers have access to clients that are attractive to many other industries. Befriend these professionals. Continuous contacts with referral sources

Orphan Clients

In every industry I've ever worked, the company had a list of prior sales where the agent had left the organization. Ask for these and introduce yourself. Many times, you will find sales opportunities.

Unsold or Aged Lead Follow-Up

Never let a prospect go completely dead. Even though you might not be able to call a client continuously, you can still email, mail, or have them in your drip campaigns. Keep them in the mix until they buy or tell you to quit contacting them.

Cold Calls Still Work

In today's selling environment, there are so many ways to get leads and find prospective customers. Many sales professionals will create a mix of as many prospecting channels as possible.

One of the oldest and most successful ways is with outbound calls, whether that is from a lead list, association list, or the good old-fashioned cold calls to businesses. The key to the success of a call is in how you present yourself and to use the same process each and every time. Consistency is incredibly important.

Here is a sequence you can adapt to your business for lead generation through outbound phone calls:

Outbound Call Steps

Open in a Positive Way
Identify Yourself and Your Company
Tell them the Reason for Your Call
Make a Value Statement, or ask a Qualifying Question
Set an Appointment for a Full Presentation

Open in a Positive Way

The opening statement should be something that elicits a positive response. People will respond in kind to the opening statement. This means a stupid question will get a stupid response. A gimmick statement will get a sarcastic response. A positive statement using the prospect's name will get a positive response.

"Good afternoon, Mr. Jones!"

Identify Yourself and Your Company

Tell them your name and company name. You should also state a brief description of what the company does and the value it provides. This is your chance to give a small "commercial" of who the company is, and their specialty.

"This is Brian McKittrick from Insurance of Texas. We specialize in helping small businesses and self-employed individuals lower their health plan costs, without sacrificing care."

Tell Them the Reason for Your Call

Get down to brass taxes as to why you're calling, or what you're calling about. There is a mutual benefit to having them know what you do so they can decide if yours is a call worth taking. For the salesperson, you need to know if this is someone interested in what is being offered. By getting it out quick, it will save both people's time (and subsequently, money). The reason for this call to get an appointment for you to present your offer. That's it for now. This is a minor commitment, versus a major commitment of getting into a pitch right then and there.

"The reason I'm calling is to set up a time where I can show you how we are saving folks 30-60% every month."

Make a Value Statement, or ask a Qualifying Question

21 Simple Tips that will Take Your Sales to the Moon!

This is a chance to make a positive statement or ask a question that would get a positive response. This statement would be based on the reason for the call, and the value your company brings. Avoid using hyperbole or asking them a question that could lead them to giving you a sarcastic response. I am frequently saving families enough money on their health plan costs to buy a new car, but a statement like that would sound like sensationalism, and come across as lame or cringe-worthy. I state the benefit more in a more professional way.

"I'm sure that you, like most families, would enjoy some extra money in the monthly budget."

Set an Appointment

The goal of the call is not to necessarily get into a presentation. Your main goal is to get them on your calendar for a full sales presentation. It would be great to get a deal on the first call, but your main focus is to schedule a time where you have their full attention and time for your official pitch. You may be using Zoom, or a PowerPoint. Those are better to be scheduled so you have their complete commitment to hearing you out. When you set the appointment, give them a choice of morning or afternoon slot on the day you prefer. It's a best practice to not put the appointment too far out. By scheduling too far in advance, you increase the risk of them canceling your appointment, or forgetting. Be sure to send them a calendar or email verification of the appointment they just committed to.

"I have open time available on Thursday. Which is better for you: 10 am or 3pm?"

Putting it all together:

"Good afternoon, Mr. Jones! This is Brian McKittrick from Insurance of Texas. We specialize in helping small businesses and self-employed individuals lower their health plan costs without sacrificing care. The reason I'm calling is to set up a time where I can show you how we are saving folks 30-60% every month. I'm sure that you, like most families, would enjoy some extra money in the monthly budget."

(Positive Response)

"That's great! I have open time available on Thursday. Which is better for you: 10 am or 3pm?"

Takeaways:

- **Classic prospecting materials and channels still work.**
- **Social media is a powerful tool for attracting clients. Choose your target platform and work it daily.**
- **Mixing multiple prospecting techniques is a strategy to get your services in front of more people in the spaces they are looking for your services.**

Sales Statistic: Over 70% of marketers rank new customers' acquisition as the top priority in their social strategy.

Research of over 11,000 marketers reveals the top priorities in increasing their ROI by social media marketing after the pandemic's initial impact. One of the biggest goals for any sales organization is to keep the pipeline filled with a steady flow of new prospects. It may not be as fun as closing a sale, but being the first step in the process, maintain motivation for prospecting is critical for attaining your sales goals.

21 Simple Tips that will Take Your Sales to the Moon!

Exercise: Properly set up your social media profiles to prepare yourself for prospecting online.

The social media preparation checklist is available at: <u>book.itaintrocketsurgery.net</u>

*Link to targeted list building database:
https://www.dataaxleusa.com/

21 Simple Tips that will Take Your Sales to the Moon!

Chapter 14 - Dress the Part: Appearance matters

"We used to have a casual dress code but too many people mistook our office for a homeless shelter."

21 Simple Tips that will Take Your Sales to the Moon!

"It IS possible to do all of these things you want IF you are willing to do the work. If you are willing to be honest with yourself about your strengths and use them to your full advantage. If you are prepared to find new solutions to the problems you are avoiding."

Jessica Denehy, CEO of Pivot and Slay Consulting and bestselling author of "Pivot and Slay"

Purpose: In this chapter, we discuss the importance of dressing appropriately for our sales position and industry.

Appearance is the first factor in appearing attractive to others. The first thing anyone will ever notice about you is your appearance, and this is their everlasting first impression. Your appearance is determined mostly by the type of clothing that you wear. Your clothing should reflect and give the impression both of who you are (personal style) and who you want to be (your position).

You have probably heard the phrase "Dress for Success" many times. I think the assumption is that dressing for success means a three-piece suit or a ballroom gown. Or your office may have a dress code that makes you look like Jake from State Farm ("Uh... Khakis!"). The reality is that you don't have to dress to the nines to look professional, nor do you have to succumb to a lame uniform that makes you feel like a cog in the corporate machine. You can have your own style and still be taken seriously.

For me, dressing the part plays a major mental role. It helps me in my head to conceptualize my roles on the sales floor. I didn't grow up in a white-collar home, but over the years held many jobs where our work attire was shirt and tie, and in some cases, suit required. When I first sold cars, our location required that we wore a dress shirt and tie (in Texas, which is brutal outside in the summer). This was a major shift for me, so I embraced it. What I noticed what that my own perception of myself was elevated, so I performed better. Years later, when I started my insurance career, I kept the mentality that I should be wearing a shirt and tie. That's when the Mr. Rogers-style sweater over the shirt and tie first showed up. It made me feel more professional, but more importantly, it made my clients feel more like they were dealing with a guy who knew what was going on. Despite being the only one at the office I worked at that wore a tie, I kept at it. Now I will never say there is something powerful in the combination of a cardigan and a tie, but it made a difference for me. And those guys could make fun of me all they wanted; instead, I embraced the look and even made a character out of it.

You can see my cartoon graphic in the link below:

https://bit.ly/cartoonbriankhaki

Benefits of Dressing for Success

Self-Confidence

One of the many benefits of dressing for success is the ability to gain self-confidence and elevate your self-esteem. It is a known fact that those who look good often feel good about themselves. When we dress up, we give ourselves a mental boost that is very important to our health and wellbeing. This added confidence is essential in instances of personal meetings with prospects, networking events, or everyone's favorite sales meetings. In these cases, that boost in the way we see ourselves can help you make a good impression.

Professional Perception

Dressing for success is often associated with professional clothes and the ability to improve your professionalism, both inside and outside of work. If the public perception of professionalism is important to you, you will want to take steps to ensure that you are dressing for success. That is why many men and women make the decision to dress for success when they attend charity events or other social parties, as well as when attending business meetings, business trips, job interviews, or in some cases, just work in general. If you just want to elevate your professional image, you don't really need to have a reason. Even if you have no one to impress, you can still benefit, in terms of self-confidence and self-esteem, from positioning yourself for success just by dressing for it.

It Goes Beyond Just Clothing

When it comes to dressing for success, a large amount of focus is placed on clothing, such as the women wearing elegant pants suits or dresses that can be worn in the office, or men, who tend to focus on business suits or dress pants. While it is important that you consider these types of clothing, you may also want to look beyond the clothing. A good percentage of your focus in the dress for success should also be placed on accessories. Common clothing accessories could include jewelry, hair accessories, belts, shoes, as well as purses, or handbags.

When it comes to accessories, you will find that you have a number of different options, particularly for women, but there are a number of accessories that men can also benefit from as well. With a little bit of shopping or researching online, you can easily find that men have just as many accessory options as women do.

Men should have

Matching dress shoes and belts, both in black and brown. Match the shoes and belt to the outfit color.

A watch. It doesn't have to be a Rolex; it could be something as simple as a Fit-Bit, or an Apple watch. A watch helps tie the ensemble together.

Men should have many tie options in nearly all colors. A tie should fit with the shirt color, then the pants and jacket. It's an entire color scheme approach. It's also helpful not to wear the same one every day.

Women should have

It's a good idea to have shoes, handbags, and accessories that match the outfit color, but also consider that you may want to purchase a number of accessories that are neutral colors. For instance, a black, brown, or off-white handbag or belt will likely go with a number of different outfits. The same can be said for shoes, jewelry, and other clothing accessories. That leopard print bag may look cool, but how universal is it? This is the office, not the club, okay?

Common Mistakes

When it comes to dressing for success, many men and women find it to be easier said than done. When dressing for

21 Simple Tips that will Take Your Sales to the Moon!

success, there are a number of factors that need to be taken into consideration, such as your gender, your reasons for wanting to improve your appearance, as well as your budget.

One of the biggest mistakes made by those looking to dress for success is assuming that the hottest items in the fashion world will make them successful (this is not always true). Fashion comes in a number of different formats. It also depends on your main purpose for looking to improve your appearance. What's trending in "Cosmo" may not have the same appeal if you are interested in appearing more professional at work. You can use fashion magazines and fashion shows as guides, but you are urged not to depend on them fully. Last I saw, the Kardashian's are filmed in their houses, not a corporate board room.

Another common mistake made by those who are looking to improve their appearance is believing that they have to have the best; the best thought to be the most expensive clothes and clothing accessories made by well-known designers. This is just not the case. Unless you want, you can choose to spend more money to wear the clothing of a professional designer, but you don't have to. Whether you are looking to dress for success for work or for an important event, it is important to remember that you do have a number of options, some of which are much more affordable.

Buying items that coworkers have is another common mistake made by those who are looking to improve their appearance. Of course, it is okay to buy clothing pieces that are similar in nature to ones that your coworkers are wearing, but you will want to avoid buying the exact same items. This is more important for women but applies to both men and women. Copying the fashions of your coworkers, right down to the same colors, can create some unneeded workplace tension.

Dressing Up on a Budget

Whether you would like to make a good impression at work, job interview, look professional and successful for an important business meeting, you may soon start shopping for new clothes. When it comes to dressing professionally, it is easy to get carried away, which might be tough if you are on a budget.

There are a few places other than the mall or boutiques that you can visit in order to stretch your dollar:

Discount Retailers

Places like Ross or TJ Maxx have strong selections of dress clothes at reasonable pricing. You will be able to find designer brand merchandise far cheaper than the department stores. I'm sure there is a reason for this, but I've never found fault in buying slacks at Ross versus Nordstrom. And these are the real brands. It's not like the label says "Paula" instead of Polo, or "Tammy Hufinger" instead of Tommy Hilfiger. For the ladies, these are great places to shop. You can also find great buys at bulk sales stores like Costco or Sam's. These would usually be the more uniform business casual items, such as polo-style shirts, oxford button-downs, and khaki dress pants at great prices. These always seem to be in stock.

Used Clothing

Thrift stores can be great ways to save money, though you will generally have trouble with the sizes. More and more, we are seeing higher-end used stores popping up. Stores like

21 Simple Tips that will Take Your Sales to the Moon!

Plato's Closet are places that pay for designer used clothing, so you have a nicer selection to shop from.

Internet Sales

If you know your measurements well, you can find fantastic buys online. The online outlets for stores like Macy's and The Gap offer deeply discounted sales. You will need to be mindful of getting the correct size, but this can be a great way to save money or make your budget go further. We also see custom-tailored websites offer clothes to your exact measurements. They have apps and tools they use to get your sizes; then you can buy the clothes that fit you like a glove.

Tips for Men

Elevating your daily dress doesn't have to be a huge jump. You can easily look better by having your clothes properly fitted. It's a small investment to go to a tailor and get your measurements. From there, buy sizes that fit your body instead of hanging off it. An inexpensive dress shirt that fits properly will look far nicer than a high-end shirt that is baggy. Same for slacks and suit jackets. Even if you are in a sales position that has a uniform, like khaki pants with a company polo, you can elevate the look by buying khaki-colored dress slacks and wearing nice dress shoes instead of something a postal worker would wear.

Tips for Women

In my option, ladies have the most options when it comes to dressing up for success, and the outfits can be repurposed so much. What usually works best is to lean toward classic and traditional designs that don't go out of style. Neutral and solid colors tend to be exempt from trends dying. Wearing shoes that are comfortable plus till classy usually ties the ensemble, and they can be repurposed in many ways.

Whatever you approach, be practical and use common sense. Dressing for success doesn't have to be a monumental shift, and a few tweaks here and there go a long way.

Takeaways:

- **Match your business outfit to suit your industry. High-ticket sales offices are usually more upscale. Transactional offers, like retail or car sales, can be more dressed-down.**
- **Avoid common mistakes like going over the top and being too trendy.**
- **If you are shopping on a budget, great deals can be found on the net and in many retailers.**

Sales Statistic: First impressions - When making a first impression, 55% is how you look, 38% is how you sound, and only 7% is what you say. The processing speed of your eyes is about 25 times faster than your ears. You have about 13 seconds to make a 1st impression, and people make significant judgments about you in the first 30 seconds of meeting you. Prepare for that first meeting to make a lasting positive impression.

Exercise: Evaluate how elevating your appearance can elevate your performance. Don't be afraid to stand out from the crowd.

**Find more tips on looking slick at:
book.itaintrocketsurgery.net**

Section 3 – The Sales Experience

21 Simple Tips that will Take Your Sales to the Moon!

Chapter 15 - Enthusiasm: Having an infectious energy

"Our company has a serious energy crisis! We've got plenty of gas, oil, and electricity, but we're dangerously low on enthusiasm."

21 Simple Tips that will Take Your Sales to the Moon!

"Enthusiasm is a choice, just like any other emotion or attitude. How you choose enthusiasm at any moment is by always finding the good or positive in any situation and switching your focus from any undesired situation to anything you can get in touch with the emotion of enthusiasm, it's contagious."

Melissa Barba, Home First Mortgage and bestselling author of "Awaken the Queen Within"

Purpose: In this chapter, we take a look at the need to be enthusiastic in what you do.

I've seen it written that "Sales is a transfer of enthusiasm." In order to be a successful salesperson, you must remain positive and enthusiastic. I've never seen Debbie Downer win a trophy for top seller. Partially because that's a fake name, but also because you can't close on negativity. You hear that, Negative Nancy?

There has been a lot of content put out over the years on enthusiasm. So much, in fact, you could probably have an entire section in the library (remember those?) just on enthusiasm, positivity, and motivation. Many of the great writers have a quote on enthusiasm:

Ralph Waldo Emerson wrote, "Enthusiasm is the mother of effort, and without it nothing great was ever achieved."

Norman Vincent Peale wrote, "Enthusiasm ... spells the difference between mediocrity and accomplishment." The list goes on and on.

Alexander Hamilton wrote, "There is a certain enthusiasm in liberty, that makes human nature rise above itself, in acts of bravery and heroism."

It's very easy to maintain enthusiasm when the cards are being dealt your way, but when the tides turn and challenges arise, that's when we face the true test of how we can remain positive. You must be prepared for things to go the other way from time to time. Enthusiasm in sales is an absolute must-have skill.

Here are ways to keep your enthusiasm high:

1. Picture the end result.

Visualizing yourself overcoming a challenge or seeing the goal being accomplished will help keep your head in the game during a storm. Keeping your focus on success will help get you through your current struggle.

2. Minimize stress.

Make an active effort to reduce your stress. Stress can cause you to dwell on your struggles. If you're too focused on your struggles, you'll have more trouble getting out of them, which will diminish your enthusiasm. Being as stress-free as possible will give you better clarity to be an enthusiastic person.

3. Stay focused.

Work on maintaining your focus (with steps in the next chapter). You'll find that it's easier to sustain enthusiasm when you know the direction in which you're headed. Focus helps you minimize struggles and can help you overcome small roadblocks.

4. Embrace the Mundane

If you allow your life to fall into a stagnant pattern, that can be a real struggle. But if you make the realization that there will be mundane crap in your position, just get it done. I saw a story about a very wealthy man, and he said the key was to do the boring tasks to perfection. Riches came from fun, but wealth comes from the mundane. You can vary how you do them, but they still must get done. You can keep the enthusiasm going with fresh thinking.

5. Stop the procrastination

It's important to keep yourself moving in order to maintain enthusiasm. If you feel that procrastination is creeping in, take some action. Taking action can get your enthusiasm back.

6. Keep an open mind

Never close your mind to new ideas and new ways of operating. Creative thinking is often accompanied by enthusiasm. Successful men and women that are creative thinkers are also wildly enthusiastic. Imagine Picasso as the Tasmanian Devil.

7. Let the little things go

I once had a regional manager in retail that would say, "Is this a hill you want to die on?" What he meant by that was, "Are you willing to waste brainpower and energy on such a little thing?" It might not seem little to us, but if this is a thing that can be eliminated, and business will not suffer, then let it go. If, in the long run, this little setback will not matter, then move forward past it. Feeling successful is from conquering great struggles.

If you have lost enthusiasm and want to get it back, the mystery to solve is within us. We can all reignite our enthusiasm by getting in touch with ourselves. That may sound like touchy-feely stuff, but what I mean is to reflect on what got you fired up to begin with. That needs to be felt again. If heavy thought, meditation, or prayer does not unlock it, then I would recommend attending a self-empowerment seminar, reading a good book that moves you, or enrolling in a mastermind group of some kind. We are all different, so find what moves you. If you have to think about that, it's okay. Most people don't know what motivates them.

There is a power that is within you as you go out into the world. Your enthusiasm existed all along inside you. You can accomplish the goals you put your mind to, and it's enthusiasm that makes the difference. We all benefit by being enthusiastic about something that we currently find boring. You may also notice that the fire of our enthusiasm may soon spread to other people.

21 Simple Tips that will Take Your Sales to the Moon!

Takeaways:

- **Sales is a transfer of enthusiasm about your product or service.**
- **Find ways to keep excited about your day today.**
- **If you have been in your role for a while, remember what got enthused in the beginning.**

Sales Statistic: 53% of consumers believe their online research is superior to interaction with a salesperson.
The generation of new prospects and buyers doesn't rely only on the efforts of salespeople as much. The way to combat this perception is to not only be an expert on what your offer is, being fanatically excited about it is something that is hard to reproduce in their own research.

Exercise: Evaluate the language you use with your clients during a sales call. Is it exciting, or does it make Mr. Rogers look like the Tasmanian Devil?

Find more exciting sales tools at:
book.itaintrocketsurgery.net

21 Simple Tips that will Take Your Sales to the Moon!

Chapter 16: The Building Blocks of Sales

21 Simple Tips that will Take Your Sales to the Moon!

"Often, getting to the next level or getting to the next stage of your life requires ending something or releasing something. Successful people know when to stop, when to let go, and then to move forward."

Wayne Salmans, Business Consultant at Hero Nation and bestselling author of "The Art of Getting Back Up"

Purpose: In this chapter, we distinctly define the steps in the sales process

The Building Blocks of Sales

1. Greeting
2. Qualification/Building rapport/Identifying Needs
3. Presentation
4. Demonstration (if applicable)
5. Trial Close
6. Overcoming objections
7. Close
8. Add-on sales
9. Asking for/Receiving referrals
10. Building repeat business

Now that we are looking at the sales profession as an entrepreneur, no matter what our level of experience, we will look at the steps to a successful sale. Each step is a building block to a new client.

There is a basic science to selling that is covered in this chapter. Throughout the chapter, I will refer to the above stages as building blocks. Every successful sale follows a logical progression, with each stage building upon the previous one, ultimately culminating in a successful sale.

I am making some basic assumptions that each of you are familiar with basic sales jargon and techniques and are comfortable approaching and talking to customers. I am also assuming that you have invested time in acquiring product knowledge and are aware of the things that make your company unique. Use those tools in every presentation, as they will help to quickly establish yourself as an expert and set you apart from the competition.

This chapter is not designed to cover every possible situation or conversation that could possibly transpire, only to familiarize you with the building blocks of the sale. My goal is that after reading this, you can readily identify which stage of the sales process you are currently in. Please take the time to learn and internalize the building blocks, and each time you are involved in the sale process, strive to be aware of which stage you are currently in, and what step the sale must progress to next.

Building Block 1 - The Greeting

Your sales conversations should start with a warm and positive greeting. Your opening line should be an open-ended question that requires a response other than a simple "Yes" or "No" answer. Avoid common canned greetings like, "May I help you?" An effective greeting for a retail or physical storefront is, "What brings you in today?" This is solid, but it can also get plenty of smart-ass comments. Try to be a bit more creative in your approach. If you are

21 Simple Tips that will Take Your Sales to the Moon!

answering the phone, a powerful question is, "What made you decide to reach out?"

Building Block 2 - Building Rapport

Whatever response you get to an open-ended question, the key is to let them talk. The prospect is very likely to give you a massive amount of information upfront that can help you craft the ideal solution. You need to also listen for ways to build rapport with the buyer. Rapport building is simply finding common ground with them and beginning to build a relationship. Rapport can be defined as that feeling people get when they like and respect a person they're speaking with. Establishing rapport is incredibly important in all phases of the sales process, and the basis of establishing trust with potential clients.

Tips for Quickly Creating Rapport

1. Be positive, but genuine
It's so damn obvious when you're being flattering or trying to butter them up. Going overboard will work against you.

2. Choose topics carefully
The last thing you want to do when you're trying to create rapport is to get into an argument. Talk about their favorite subject: them! Topics like family are easy, or their business. Avoid topics with high emotional triggers such as politics and religion.

3. Express genuine interest
If you're asking someone questions, be present in the moment and listen to their answers. Lean forward a little, nod your head occasionally, and acknowledge what they are saying. This will communicate to them that you're listening and interested.

4. Get a laugh
Making someone laugh is enormous in getting someone to like you. We tend to find people that make us laugh more favorable to be around. You don't have to be "on stage" the whole time you're talking with someone, but if you can make an occasional joke or share a funny anecdote, this will help create a more likable experience for the sales process. Safe jokes can be made about yourself or the situation you're in. Avoid criticism or negative talk about others.

5. Watch and Listen for the way they are sharing information.
You need to take notice of whether they communicate in visual, auditory, or kinesthetic descriptions, which is a fancy way to say hearing, seeing, or doing. Matching their style will build trust. Listen for phrases such as:

"I see your point"
"I hear what you're saying"
"I feel the same way?"

You also should try to mirror the way that they are carrying themselves, in tone and inflection of speech. You don't want to make this obvious, but it's very helpful to match their pose and alter your way of speaking slightly to match theirs. Don't try to add an accent if you don't have one. Being a near lifelong Texan, I deeply appreciate a good accent, but I don't speak with one, and I don't fake it either. I realize that I have a tendency to talk fast, and if I'm dealing with a slower speaking prospect, I will be careful to take my time. However, I say, and even type, the word "Y'all" no matter what the scenario!

21 Simple Tips that will Take Your Sales to the Moon!

Building Block 3 - Qualification | Identifying Needs

This is the stage of the sale where you identify needs, ask pointed questions designed to help you make a recommendation, and begin to gain the customer's trust. It is an unusual experience for the customer to be shown courtesy, personal attention, and genuine concern for their needs from a salesperson.

If you do something unusual, you have the ability to change belief systems. If you change a customer's belief that all salespeople are "out to get them," you will be able to quickly gain the customer's trust and build rapport. By asking meaningful questions, asking for their opinion, and finding common ground, you are giving them a reason to trust you. By doing these unusual things, you do more to earn their trust, earn their business, or even make a larger sale to them in a shorter period of time.

When identifying the needs of a client, imagine the process as a funnel. As you ask questions, you are narrowing it down to the one or two products or services that fit their needs and budget. At the top of the funnel, you are asking general questions. As the funnel narrows, your questions get more specific until you can pinpoint the exact solution. As you ask questions, what you are really looking for doing is eliminating what they WON'T BUY. If you sold cars, you would ask a prospective buyer what color car they want in the very beginning. That's too narrow at first. The first thing you would need to find out is what type of vehicle they were looking for: car, truck, van, bus, dune buggy, etc. Then get more specific with benefits they need; finally, you narrow down to the small things like color.

Do you have a script for your qualifying process?

This is the standard questionnaire I use with ALL health insurance prospects. I have used this thousands of times, and it is done without fail for all new leads. You want to internalize your regular format. Do not deviate from what works once you have it down.

1. I get their name, and use it often
2. Contact Info: Phone and Email
3. Is this a plan for yourself or for a family?
4. Resident Zip Code (county)
5. Are they currently covered: If so, get the carrier and premium
6. What is the age or date of birth for each person to be covered?
7. Do you have an ongoing medical need?
8. Do you take any medicines regularly?
9. Do you use tobacco (vape)?
10. Some of the plans offer a premium discount based on household income. What is your annual income?
Lastly, what's your favorite dinosaur?

This is a joke, but you should see the responses I get from people in messages and emails. Gotta have some fun with it, too.

One key during the qualification process is to be present in the moment. You MUST listen intently to what they are saying. The information you are gathering is essentially "the answers to the test," if you will. When going through your questions to the prospects, you must eliminate distractions:

Put your cell phone away
Use a cheat sheet, and if necessary, take notes
Put notes in your CRM
Repeat statements, and ask questions to clarify needs
Listen to what they are saying.

21 Simple Tips that will Take Your Sales to the Moon!

Makes qualifying easier
What's their HOT button?
A "hot button" is the benefit or feature that your prospect is most interested in. There is a pain point, and the hot button is the way to eliminate that pain (in their understanding). Once you uncover what's most important to them in order to fill their need or fix a problem, you need to highlight this benefit as much as possible throughout the rest of the sales conversation.

Building Block 4 - Presentation

After you have a clear mental understanding of what your prospect is looking for, with a precise understanding of their needs and budget, now is the time to give a presentation of what the best fit for them will be in your product or service offering.

At the beginning of the presentation, you want to start with just a slice of the overview of the industry. This may not apply to all offerings, but most sales pros can begin this way. It doesn't have to be monumental, just a brief description of where your market is today and what's out there. Then you want to make the recommendation of what you feel their best choice would be. Remember, there is power in the words you choose to say. I always start with, "For your needs, I would recommend…" By starting with that brief overview, you are implying there are multiple options, and then by presenting the one option that fits them best, you are making it personal. If you have done all the steps of the sales process correctly and professionally up to this point, you will be seen as an expert. So, what they are about to hear is the opinion of an expert in the field. The next step is to describe in detail the product or service that fits their needs. But your description should always be benefit-based. Features cost money, but benefits provide value. When you rattle off a list of features, the client is only seeing the price going up. But when you present a benefit and tell the client what it will do for them to make their life better or easier, then you are elevating their perceived value. Your presentation should be based on highlighting the benefits that your client holds most important, aka their "hot button(s)."

In some cases, you may have more than one choice for the prospect. If that is the case, present a high-level view of each one, then describe each one in detail in an either-or type of conversation. After that, you'll want to plainly ask them, "Which option is sounding better to you?" Be direct.

You'll want to use questions throughout the presentation that require feedback from the customer. Use open-ended questions (trial closes) that will elicit a "yes" response and encourage the customer to talk more. If the customer is talking, they are buying. Remember, many small "yeses" throughout the presentation make the large "YES!" at the close much easier for the customer. Selling is not telling. Interact with your audience. Your presentation should be rehearsed, but not robotic. This is an opportunity to transfer enthusiasm about your product or service, so have energy.

Tie the Prospect's Needs to the Presentation:

Power Statement:
"Because you said you needed (necessary benefit), I'd recommend this (plan or item that has that benefit)."

Here's an example of what I mean:

"Because you said pregnancy is still a goal, and you travel across the country, I'd recommend the OneShare Complete plan that covers maternity, has an unlimited number of doctor visits, and has a nationwide PPO network under

21 Simple Tips that will Take Your Sales to the Moon!

Aetna that will allow you to visit doctors around the country in that network."

Hot Buttons: Pregnancy | Travel

Benefits: Maternity | National Network

Present the Benefits they Mentioned:

Needs and Benefits. Put them together; then babies come out... I mean, sales come out!

Other tips when presenting to a client:

Use a Brochure. You aren't expected to be an encyclopedia, and it will give you the opportunity to highlight key points relevant to your prospective client.
Stand Up (if you are commonly in a desk position)
Look out a window if you are on a phone presentation. This will take your mind's eye off what you normally are looking at, and you can create a mental picture of the prospect.
You cannot present every option you have and expect them to make a buying decision.
Ideally, present one option, two at most (either/or). The more options they see, the longer it will take them to decide on how to move forward.

Building Block 5 - Demonstration (if applicable)

If you are in an industry that has physical products, such as cars or retail stores, the demonstration can be one of the most fun parts of the sales process. This is the chance to play with the toys we sell to prospects. When I sold cars, I looked forward to getting a client behind the wheel so they could get that excitement. I never understood when some folks were not interested in taking a test drive. In all sales cases, this is the moment when a potential client can experience themselves owning your product. This can be the part of the sale that may make or break the deal. If you have had a fantastic presentation, your product demonstration will need to live up to the hype, or maybe your presentation was mundane, but a great demo may put them over the edge.

There is a simple and effective way to provide a fantastic demonstration:

<u>Predict</u> - Tell them what the experience will be like; what to look and listen for.

<u>Prove</u> - Have the product perform to the best of its ability. Make sure you are prepared ahead of time. Practice your demonstration skills.

<u>Confirm</u> - Make sure they experience what you told them to be looking and listening for.

<u>Blame it on the gear</u> - The product is the star. Tell them what is special about your product that made the experience enjoyable.

Doing your demonstration, make sure you watch your prospect. Most in-store demos are ninety (90) seconds or less. For a car test drive, there is a lot more time. Watch them like a hawk.

Are they getting it?
Is it blowing their hair back?
What part are they digging the most?

Building Block 6 - Trial Closes

If you have done everything correctly up until this point, then what follows here is the easy part. You should expect that the customer would buy! After all, you have built rapport, gained their trust, and made a recommendation for them to buy based upon the information they have provided you. However, this is the part that most salespeople stumble on. Don't let fear cause you not to ask for the sale. If you have done everything above, you are entitled to ask for the sale! This stage is your first closing attempt. But you may still need to come to terms. This is why I call this a trial close. You absolutely want to ask them if they agree that this is the product or service that fits their needs; if they want to move forward with your offer, then proceed to finalizing the purchase.

If you have landed on the wrong product or service for them, they should be letting you know. Do not be afraid to dig to find the real solution. You may have missed something, or it is possible that you don't offer what they truly need. That's perfectly fine. It's never a good idea to force something on a prospect that doesn't fully meet their needs as a solution.

Ideally, you have the proper product or service for them. If they are not buying immediately, you then need to proceed to coming to the terms and conditions on which they will buy. This may require some negotiation, but that is the best part. Any reason the potential customer gives you for not taking action today is actually the condition or circumstance that you can overcome in order for them to buy from you. It's really their perfect terms. The next thing to do is handle those objections like a pro.

Building Block 7 - Overcoming Objections

We will cover this building block topic in detail in Chapter Eighteen (18)

Building Block 8 - The Close

We will cover this building block topic in detail in Chapter Nineteen (19).

Building Block 9 - Add-on Sales

Add-ons, accessories, or ancillary items are designed to enhance the performance of your main product or service. In most cases, the main item doesn't function as well without having some type of enhancement item to go along with it. So, selling a complete package to your customers is not to add commissions to your pocketbook, but it provides a complete solution to the customer as well. You could be doing the customer a disservice by not presenting them everything they need to fully enjoy their product.

Here are some examples of add-ons that make a difference:

Cables to connect devices to a TV
Power supplies in Audio-Video Systems
Audio upgrades
Furniture upgrades
Performance parts added to a car sale
Wear and Tear protection added to an auto lease
Extra coverages such as accident and illness protection plans for insurance
Strap, picks, and strings for guitars

There are countless examples, but the point I am making is that you need to be prepared to offer more than just your main item.

Don't beat around the bush and present add-ons first. I've seen this be a problem for inexperienced salespeople. The proper thing is to mention these during the presentation and

21 Simple Tips that will Take Your Sales to the Moon!

demonstration stages. If early in the presentation, the seed was planted for add-ons, then once the main item has been selected, now it is time to harvest the plant that has sprouted. Go into your presentation of add-ons. You have the prospect's permission, they need the add-ons, and you have built trust and rapport, so this should be easy. It's easier to sell down than up, so a full solution presentation has a higher success rate at this point than starting from scratch at the presentation phase on each new product you wish to add to the sale. Remember, don't stop selling what they will need until the customer stops buying.

Building Block 10 - Asking for/Receiving Referrals

This is the second most important thing you can do to ensure long-term success in this business. By asking for and receiving referrals, you are "keeping the pipeline full" of new prospects at all times. Referrals are also much easier to build rapport with as they have been recommended by someone they trust, so they will trust you as well. Look at everyone as a potential source of referrals:

Existing customers
Potential customers
Family/Friends
Waiters
Vendors
Corporate reps and sponsors
Salespeople in other industries
Delivery personnel
Mailmen
Other business owners you do business with.
And a huge resource is your contact list in social media.

Remember, everyone has a "circle of influence," and if they remember you as someone who does business in an unusual way, they will recommend you as an expert who can be trusted.

Asking for and receiving referrals separates the champions from the also-rans.

The group most likely to give you the best referrals is your top 20% of customers. They will be your biggest cheerleaders to their circle of influence. If you ask them, they will be happy to provide you with names and contact information of other potential prospects who are likely themselves going to become part of your top 20% of customers. Remember, people associate with other people like themselves.

Once you have received the referral, it is important to do two things:

Promptly contact the referral
Use the referrer's name as the source

Be sure to send the person who gave you the referral a thank you message or card, and let them know that you took care of the referral.

Building Block 11 - Building Repeat Business

Building repeat business is about creating brand loyalty. I believe that this is the most important thing you can do to survive in this business. Building a large customer base ensures that you will have a steady flow of income even during slow times. Remember the 80/20 rule:

80% of your business will come from 20% of your customers.

21 Simple Tips that will Take Your Sales to the Moon!

Let's look at a few tips to build client relationships and repeat business:

1. The first step in building repeat business is to make a conscious decision to do everything in your power to give the customer a WOW experience, a reason to remember you, and a reason to want to shop with you again.

2. Verbally thank the customer for their purchase, give them your contact information, and tell them: "Please give me a call if you have any questions, if you experience any problems, or if I can be of any assistance in the future."

3. Ask them for feedback. Why they purchased today, and what you could do to improve your presentation. People love to be asked for their opinion and will be flattered that you asked.

4. Give them a follow-up call to make sure that they are happy with their purchase. If they are not, make it right. If they are, remind them that they can call you if they require any assistance in the future.

5. Send them a handwritten thank you note with your name and contact information. In many cases, a personalized gift will be huge, depending on your average sale price, and pending any industry regulations.

6. Promptly take care of any problems they have, or if you made a mistake. If you immediately rectify a bad situation- you have a customer for life.

7. Remember not only your customer's names, but special events in their lives. Regular contact during special days can go a long way, such as emails on birthdays and holidays.

8. If you see a newsworthy item that relates to your customer, or his business, send them a message. They will be happy you remembered them.
9. Never, ever, never break a promise, or forget to call a customer back.

10. Once a year, send a mailing out to the top 20% of your customers thanking them for their patronage and being a large part of your success. Around Christmas season seems to work the best and have the most impact.

Doing most, or some, of the suggestions in the above 10 items, will ensure that customers will return time and again and that they will always look for you when they need what you sell.

Takeaways:

- **If you study the preceding information, and use the building block approach to every sale, your income can only go one direction: Up!**

- **There is a definite science to selling-it is a learned skill. In this chapter, I have only covered a small portion of the basics of salesmanship. Being a sales champion takes hard work and dedication. In order to progress as a salesperson, you need to focus on continually improving your skillset. To that end, I highly recommend that you read books, listen to motivational tapes, and attend seminars that are centered around sales. Effort expended towards being a sales champion is never wasted. It shows results almost immediately in the areas of increased sales, greater job satisfaction, and more money in your pocket.**

21 Simple Tips that will Take Your Sales to the Moon!

Sales Statistic: Here are the top ways to create a positive sales experience, according to buyers:

Listen to their needs (69%)
Don't be pushy (61%)
Provide relevant information (61%)
Respond in a timely manner (51%)

Listen to what buyers are telling you, and adjust your sales process accordingly. After all, they are the ones paying you for what you're doing.

Exercise: Clearly articulate the steps in your sales process, and what step you are best at, and which step is costing you sales because you are not executing properly.

"Step" on over to book.itaintrocketsurgery.net for the sales process guide

21 Simple Tips that will Take Your Sales to the Moon!

Chapter 17 -– Value: Selling on what's really important

"You're a pretty good sales rep, except for the nine times you called me 'wallet' instead of 'Walter'."

21 Simple Tips that will Take Your Sales to the Moon!

"Not all reinventions are the results of traumatic life events, like divorce or loss. There are times when you just want to know if there is something 'more interesting' to try your hand at."

Nancy Meek, Co-Founder of Women 360 and bestselling author of "Ignite the Fire Within"

Purpose: In this chapter, we discuss how value in the product or service is what people will treasure

Sell on value, not on price!

This is a staple catchphrase used by every sales manager in history. But on this one, let's give them a pass, because it is as true a statement as there has ever been stated in the sales game. It is so true, in fact, that it would be considered one of the ten commandments of sales.

At what point does a sale take place?

A lot of sales professionals would probably say that a sale happens when money changes hands or when a client takes delivery. This may be true of the sales transaction to be completed, but in actuality, a sale happens when the prospect's perceived value of the product/service exceeds the price. Think about that for just a moment.

How many times in your life have you saved money for something you wanted to buy?

Saving up $700 for a new Beretta 9mm
Saving up $1,500 for a new Fender Stratocaster
Saving up $5,000 for a professional mentor program (BFA Apex)
Saving up $100,000 for a top-of-the-line Cadillac
Saving up the down payment on a $500,000 log cabin in Utah

We've all done this. If there is a point in wanting to put together the "scratch" to buy an item, then we've already been closed, or closed ourselves, on having our dream (insert thing). We see the value. We want it. If the money was there, we'd already have it. Sales will be lost on customers not being able to make the payment, but the price they are willing to pay is determined by the perceived value they have established in the product or service at the end of the presentation.

Sell on the value of product benefits, not on justifying the price

In order to build value, you must discuss the benefits of your product or service. Benefits have value; features cost money. If you are just rattling off a series of features, then all you are doing is driving up the price in the customer's mind. Stating the benefit of what the feature does and tying that benefit to the client's needs will build value.

Here's a story about value:

As a member of a professional mentor program called Apex (by Break Free Academy), we occasionally have meetings. At my very first meeting, I sat with three successful men.

21 Simple Tips that will Take Your Sales to the Moon!

During our light dinner, these three fellas were talking about the cost and logistics of owning a private jet. There was only one moment in which the price was brought up. The rest of the conversation revolved around the benefits of owning a plane that would cost over a million dollars. If you fly often enough, having your own plane can save you a ton of time and hassle. First of all, you buy a plane in the same manner you buy a house, so you're most likely financing let's say $1,500,000. Second, let's look at the benefits: business tax write-off of the costs and depreciation - Partner with others and now you're each lowering the costs - Bypass all the crappy experience that goes along with commercial air travel - You set your schedule, instead of being at the mercy of the airlines. These are just some of the benefits received if you were to spend over a million dollars on your own plane. Cost is certainly a factor in owning your own plane; otherwise, more people would go out and buy one. But this conversation wasn't about justifying the price of a plane, it was about the value of a private plane. One concept most people don't understand is the value of time. Think to yourself of all the headaches you've had dealing with airports. Also, add up the extra time you would save, cutting out the unnecessary waiting in line to get tickets, then the boarding the plane process. By bypassing all the usual bullshit that goes along with air travel, owning your own plane is not only an upgrade in air travel, it becomes an investment in buying back the time and effort of simplifying traveling by plane. The is the nature of value exceeding price.

To visualize the idea of value exceeding price, take a look at this illustration:

Above the line = WOW! Factor

Sale happens when the value exceeds the price of the product or service

LINE: Customer Expectation | Price

Perceived Value →

Below the Line = Disappointment | Lose the Sale | Return or Cancellation

In all transactions, a customer has a "line" if you will, that represents their expectation and price about what they are shopping for. In order for the prospect to be "sold," then either the need or the value of the item must be greater than their "line." Or you must drop the price down to their value level. As a salesperson, you are the client's partner in the achievement of your client's goals. In order to do that, you need to know where they are going, and how they want to get there. Once you know those two things, it's then your job to construct the roadmap on their behalf.

To create a value proposition, which is a unique point of view from the customer about the product or service, you must know what benefit they hold in the most esteem. The key elements come from the list below, but the main value will be in what pain the customer is having, and how your product or service alleviates that pain. Creating the greatest overall value will come from understanding the right combination of appeals and by presenting the value proposition as a custom fit to the prospective customer's wants and needs. You will need to understand their decision-making process.

Product or Service Appeals that will Increase Value:

- Asset - Will the product or service have an increased monetary value?
- Ease of Use - IS the product or service easier to use than the competition?
- Information - Does the product or service provide much-needed information?
- Service - Does the product or service provide a much-needed service element?
- Stability - Does the product or service company have a long-standing track record, or reputation?
- Support - Does the product or service provide protection, which can be physical or monetary?

By highlighting the strongest appeal to your client, you are crafting your offer as their best solution.

Five (5) Ways to Sell on Value, Instead of Price:

1. Be Unique

Unique can be in a product or service that no one else has, or just being different in your approach. If you don't have a unique selling point, then be unique in how you conduct business. If there is nothing that differentiates you from your competition, you become common, and the only thing that will make you different is the price.

Look at your skillset:
Are you a specialist or an expert?
Is there something different about you or your company?

Can you harness a technology to stand out?

2. Choose Your Clients Carefully

You need to very carefully craft an avatar of what your ideal client looks and acts like. To begin controlling your business, write down the attributes of the people you want as clients and then go out and get them with targeted marketing. Get very specific on this, but the top priority should be to attract people you want to do business with. It's a tough road constantly working with clients you don't like. Have a referral partner that you can send clients that do not fit your criteria.

3. Set High Standards

Working with just anyone lowers your value. If you have a process to qualify prospects in order to work with you, then you increase your value in the eyes of your clients. Have ways to evaluate your clients for their intention to buy, timeline to move on the deal, and income qualifications, then you are elevating the quality of your offer by positioning yourself as only working with a certain stand of clients.

4. Create Value in The Eyes of Clients by Providing what no one else offers

Sales professionals are slowly being removed from the buying process. This is happening because, by and large, salespeople have not been showing clients the value they bring to the transaction, or the salesperson made the transaction more difficult. If you educate the prospect on what you have done to make the deal happen or the steps you have taken to make the sale easier for them, you will show them a glimpse of what value you are bringing. To take it a step further, if you can do something that your competition doesn't that adds value, definitely tell them about it. If no other competing business offers any of these benefits, then a client that wants to work with you must pay what you ask.

5. Provide value that no one else offers

When prospects do business with me, they get a complete outline that explains my process from start to finish. It also includes samples, a list of service providers that could be involved in the process, and much more.

6. Compete on Value, Not Price

It doesn't take any special skill, experience, or knowledge to compete on price. If you are the cheapest, then you will win the price game. But this is a game you're not really winning. In order to maintain low pricing, you must continually cut into the profit margin. If you gained a client because you were the cheapest, you would only have them as a client as long as no other competitor undercuts you. The moment someone else has a lower price, your client will jump ship. The way to get paid what you're worth is to visibly demonstrate your value to your clients. Competing on price does not create value. Reject price shoppers. Studies have shown that just over 15% of shoppers make their buying decisions based on price as the primary factor.

A Thought on Price

"It is unwise to pay too much, but it's also unwise to pay too little. When you pay too much, all you lose is a little money. But when you pay too little, you stand a chance of losing everything. Because the thing you bought is incapable of doing what you bought it to do. The common law of business balance prohibits paying a little and getting a lot; it just cannot be done. So, when you deal with the lowest bidder, it

is wise to put a little something aside to take care of the risk you run. And if you do that, you can afford something better."

John Ruskin, English Philosopher, 1819-1900

Don't forget that real professionals earn their money by helping clients maximize value, minimize costs, save time, and much more. If potential clients don't appreciate this, then feel free to refer them to a partner that will service them. To be successful, you don't need every prospect, and you certainly don't need every buyer. If all someone wants is a cheap transaction, send them to a vendor who competes on price.

Key Points to Remember About Value

1. Time as a monetary value
2. People Buy From People - Not Products or Services
3. Find Common Ground and Build Rapport
4. Every piece of the sales process is equally important
5. Do not skip steps in the sales process
6. Set the expectation in the paperwork or completion of the sale
7. Make sure you and your sales environment present a professional image - this is your office or online
8. Get customer involved in sales process
9. Have Fun - if they can laugh, then you have set yourself apart
10. Assume everybody is a buyer - they will buy from someone and somewhere at some point.

An example of building value from product or service benefits:

21 Simple Tips that will Take Your Sales to the Moon!

Let's look at a health insurance plan. Remember, the true purpose of an insurance policy is to transfer the risk of financial exposure from the client to the insurance company. Insurance is not for annual physicals being paid for or having a doctor visit copay. Insurance is for the protection of your assets and giving you peace of mind in the uncertainty of having an accident, or a major health event (such as cancer-heart attack-stroke).

Other features on a plan such as doctor visit copays, annual wellness and preventive care, or drug formularies are labeled as value-added benefits. The first priority is to protect the assets of the client in unforeseen medical costs. These other benefits should be icing on the cake, not the main reasons to buy a health plan.

Present your plans to clients based on value. If you're just talking about the features of a plan in order to justify the price, you will have a much harder time closing. Clients that have purchased on price will buy the next plan they see that is cheaper, regardless of the benefits. However, if you have presented the value in the benefits of your health plan, the client is much more likely to remain enrolled over a longer period of time. If your client believes in the value in having their health plan, when they see a cheaper plan online or in a commercial, they will likely call you to see what the difference is versus their current plan. Explain the benefit of the features in the plan in a way that shows them the value. There is no value in the price alone.

Takeaways:

- **Benefits have value, features only cost money. Find the main attraction the consumer has for your product or service, and that is what you highlight.**

- **Price is justified when the value is high enough; no matter what the item is.**

Sales Statistic: Nearly half of buyers, 47%, think an essential quality in a salesperson is "trustworthy."

One of the trends that customers are led by is that "trust gets deals done." Buyers emphasized the importance of salespeople being "trustworthy," as the top quality. A presentation based on the value in your offer, based on what was most important to your prospect, with show that you have listened in intently during the sales call. This goes a long way toward building trust.

Exercise:

To visualize value versus price, you should think of the auto industry. Let's say you're looking for a 4-door sedan. For the sake of the exercise, we're looking at new cars from American brands. You can get a base model Ford Fiesta starting around $14,000. On the Cadillac website, their top-of-the-line sedan is the CT6-V, which will cost over $100,000.

Activity: Take out a pen and paper (don't use a computer for this), and start listing the value of each car. What I think you'll find is that the Cadillac has all the benefits the Ford will give, plus adds many more. It's tempting to try to justify the $100,00 price tag, but that is not how luxury car dealers sell their vehicles. Luxury dealers build value in the benefits of owning a Cadillac. This will help you to determine the highest value in what you sell.

You can access the guide on building value at: book.itaintrocketsurgery.net

21 Simple Tips that will Take Your Sales to the Moon!

Chapter 18 – Overcoming Objections: They are really buying signals

"If you know how to turn obstacles into opportunity, why do I have to move my toys off the stairway?"

21 Simple Tips that will Take Your Sales to the Moon!

"Failure is unacceptable. It should not be an option. When you have this mindset, then the only result will be success."

Mehdi Kouchtaf, Branch Manager and Senior Loan Officer at Open Mortgage of McKinney, Texas, and bestselling author of "Foreigner in My Own World"

Purpose: In this chapter, we will outline the steps and skills needed to effectively overcome objections.

Overcoming Objections

Many salespeople cringe when they hear an objection, but that feeling needs to be flipped. If you are a salesperson who wants sales calls free of difficult questions, then you should sell cups of ice water in the desert. If you were simply an order-taker, then you would not experience the challenges of selling.

You need to see objections positively.

An objection is really a signal of a buyer. The prospect is disclosing to you a reason that is preventing them from buying, and if solved, they now have a clear path to move forward. If they were truly not interested in what you offer or incapable of buying it, then you wouldn't even hear an objection. The prospect would most likely end the conversation.

Brian McKittrick – It Ain't Rocket Surgery

The number of objections you meet on a daily basis in your particular marketplace tends to indicate the amount of value and prestige that is assigned to your position. In a general sense, salespersons are rewarded for the amount of difficulty that goes along with the problem that they are solving. Going back to the selling water in the desert example, there are no objections to overcome, so there is very little skill involved in making that sale. In comparison to a sales pro in a field that requires a high financial commitment, or a product that requires more consideration, will be better compensated. Where would you prefer to be on the commission ladder? Would you rather be on the high end, answering numerous objections throughout your day, or on the bottom, facing little to no adversity?

When I was a sales manager for a consumer electronics retailer, I stepped in to help one of my sales guys close a deal on two high-end digital video cameras that a church was buying. The church Pastor and the audio-video (AV) technician were hammering my guy on price! I have no problem making deals happen to close a deal. Negotiations and discounts aren't that common in retail much anymore, but in commission environments, you can many times get some money off if you're buying products in a package.

Brian: "Did I charge you to park in our parking lot?"

Daryl: "No, why?"

Brian: "I didn't charge you because this isn't a flea market. $2,250 each will be the best price we can do. I have them both in stock. We can take care of this now, and you can start working on your project today."

21 Simple Tips that will Take Your Sales to the Moon!

Daryl and the AV tech were taken aback, then smiled a little. With a light chuckle, Daryl said, "Okay, let's get them rung up."

Brian: "Now, have we talked about the protection plan yet…?"

The reason I got a little aggressive with Daryl was because of two things:

1. I was protecting my sales guy. If you're the leader of a group, you need to occasionally "flex" if a member of your crew is being attacked.

2. I knew Daryl and the AV tech wanted to get their project going. The VALUE was to find cameras that worked and get their project going. Haggling at another shop was just going to waste more time.

I went for the close on $2,250 because it was a total discount of $500. Also, even with the protection plans on each and sales tax, I knew it was within his budget. He had $5,000 in his pocket. I knew that because no one goes shopping with a budget of a weird number. The church gave him $5,000 to spend. Not $4,500, but also not $6,000, which was the whole reason he wanted to make a deal anyway. Daryl just wanted the best VALUE for his $5,000. Daryl saw that the cameras were exactly what they needed, so he just wanted to get the most he could for $5,000. All he had to do was tell my sales guy that. Most salespeople would think the price was the objection when the real issue was getting the value he saw in his budget.

Most consumers are not complaining about the price, but instead, what they are doing is trying to get the value they see for a certain number. As a salesperson, your job is to build value in what you are presenting past the price of the item.

The best way to overcome objections is to eliminate them from the sale throughout the process.

In Your Marketing: Your offer should attract your ideal client – generate an avatar of the perfect fit for your offer.

During Your Qualifying Questionnaire: Your information gathering should funnel prospects into the product or plan that fits their needs and budget. Find the benefit they need the most. If at all possible, add more options in what you sell to address a wide range of client budgets and needs.

During Pitch: Your presentation should highlight the benefits of your product that are the most important to your lead.

When It's Time to Overcome Objections: Your goal in overcoming any objections is not to try to convince your prospect that they are wrong. Rather, this is the chance to isolate the reason for the objection. This could be a time to educate your consumer, or maybe there is a misunderstanding at some point in your presentation. But after you isolate the objection, get a commitment that if you can solve the problem, they are ready to move forward.

You should be optimistic when you are faced with an objection or tough question. You should see this objection as an indicator that you are moving in the right direction. When a prospect voices his or her concern over a certain aspect of your product or service, this is now a chance for you to redirect your sales presentation.

21 Simple Tips that will Take Your Sales to the Moon!

Objections also give you the opportunity to hone your sales skills.

The more objections that you face and successfully conquer, the better salesperson you become. Unless the prospect's objections completely destroy your product's benefits, properly overcoming the objection gives you the best chance at closing the sale.

While objections obviously present salespeople with barriers to actually finalizing transactions, viewing these objections and tough questions in a positive light can only help you make more sales. As you start to notice patterns in the ways prospects present their objections, as well as the consistent themes in these objections, you will be able to almost predict what kinds of objections your prospects will present. You'll learn how to ask questions that help you flush them out or even eliminate them.

So, when you feel that objection coming up, get excited! That's when the real selling begins.

Isolate objections:

You cannot be attempting to close the deal with having too many objections. If you have multiple objections at the same time, then you might need to reevaluate the product or service you have presented. Most commonly, prospects object to only a few categories of objections. Have a solve for each one of these:

1. Price
2. A feature or benefit
3. Timing

1. Clarify the Objection:
"If I understand you correctly, we need to (resolve - correct - obtain) the (objection). Is that right?"

2. Get a commitment:
"If I was able to resolve (the objection), would there be anything else keeping us from moving forward?"

Example:
"So, if I understand you correctly, we need to find you a health plan for your family in your budget of being under $800. Is that right?" YES

"If I was able to get the health plan down under $800, would there be anything else keeping you from enrolling for April 1st?"

Overcome Objections Sequence:

Here is a handy word sequence you can use to bring it all together:

No problem...
I'd be happy to...
I understand...
Please allow me to...
I'm confident...
I wouldn't expect you to buy...
Would you do me a favor...
Please tell me no...

Client:
"That premium is too high.

Salesperson:

21 Simple Tips that will Take Your Sales to the Moon!

"No problem. I'd be happy to look for another option. I understand how the monthly budget is a big factor. Please allow me to find another option. I'm confident we can find a plan that meets your needs and budget. I would not expect you to buy a plan you're unhappy with. Would you do me a favor, and if we can't make it work, please tell me it's not for you."

Takeaways:

- **Prevent objections by mentioning the solutions to objections during your qualifying and presentation stage.**
- **Use the objection itself as a way to close the sale. The objection in most ways is the obstacle to overturn that will close the sale.**
- **Have answers ready to overcome your most common objections.**

"In these days, the potential customers have more options than ever before, the best competitive advantage a salesperson can have, is the ability to turn an objection to a buying sign. When a person says, "Yes, but…," all he wants is for that salesperson to fix the pain he's feeling a different way than he presented it. It is always important to start handling the objection with a positive message to show the prospect that you are on his side, and it is totally normal for him to feel a certain way. Never make him feel the way that his way is totally wrong, as you will be criticizing the ways he has been doing business for a while, make him understand that what he was doing was good, but you just have a better alternative that will get him a better a result or the same result with less cost and effort. Every industry has a handful of objections that keep coming up over 90% of the time. If you master how to handle them, you will never go broke!" -Mehdi Kouchtaf

Sales Statistic: The biggest challenges today's salespeople face:

Establishing urgency (42%)
Getting in touch with prospects (37%)
Overcoming price objections (35%)

What you think the main objection might be to your product or service is not always the case. Price might not be the most important aspect of the sale to your clients, so be ready to handle any type of pushback to the sale closing.

Exercise: What are your most common objections? Practice statements on isolating them, then your close using the objection sequence.

Download the objection sequence sheet at:
book.itaintrocketsurgery.net

21 Simple Tips that will Take Your Sales to the Moon!

Chapter 19 – The Close: Helping them make a decision

"For 35 years I tried to sign you up as a client. Now that we're both here, I've got the rest of eternity to keep trying!"

21 Simple Tips that will Take Your Sales to the Moon!

"If you are ready to take action, assume total control of your life, and excited to accelerate the process, then the only person that needs to sign off on that is you. We all get one shot at this life. Quit waiting on someone else to give you the chance, and just take it!"

Ramon Casaus, Founder of ROC Real Estate Partners and bestselling author of *"No Permission Needed"*

Purpose: In this chapter, we take a deep dive into the step of the sales process that salespeople find the most challenging

"Besides the fact that you don't like me, is there anything else that would keep you from buying this TV today?" I actually once said that to a couple. They laughed and did the deal!

The key to being a "closer" is reading the situation. You should be picking up on vibe, pace, body language, as well as what the prospect is saying out loud.

Now, this particular couple really liked the TV, had already applied for credit. They were available any time for delivery because they were retired. I could tell they just didn't click with me as a person and were getting slightly annoyed with my presentation on accessories because I had added on the extended warranty. When I picked up on their impatience, I went for the close. I said this to throw them off a bit and get a laugh. And it worked!

Closing the deal is where the rubber meets the road in sales. Closing well is the difference between getting paid or not, having chicken for dinner, or eating feathers…

But one flaw in sales is that most salespeople will put such a high mystique on the close as if it's some magical part of life that few are entrusted with its power. The truth is that it's only another step in the process. Just another piece of the transaction that sits between Presentation and Delivery.

Let's examine some ways to demystify the close and make it easier to get prospective clients to the close.

Part 1 - The Client Experience:

The first thing you need to do in order to close more deals is to actually take a thorough look at your sales process. Have you ever walked every step of your prospect-to-client experience? This is the chance to literally go to the drawing board and examine each piece of your steps the customer must go through from their perspective.

How does it look?
How does it feel?
What steps do you put them through?
Can they be streamlined?

What have you done to prepare for a customer?

Part 2 - First Impressions

Mapping out your customer experience is a very important part of the sales process; however, it is one of the most neglected. After you have your experience map, we then must dial in the quality of the first time a prospect will interact with us; in person or online. A customer's first impression of you or your company, and the way you do business, can be a great help or hindrance to closing a sale. We must make every effort to make our customer's initial impression a favorable one.

Part 3 - Present the Ideal Solution

The proper solution for a client should be the only choice to alleviate their pain points. Many below-average sales folks will offer too many choices, or they are really trying to educate prospects instead of selling them on the right product or service that solves their issue.

A great solution starts by being present and listening to what they are saying. This, in turn, makes qualifying easier. What's the HOT button? You cannot present every choice you offer and expect them to make a buying decision. Ideally, present one option, or two at most in the presentation that is an either/or fashion. The more options you present, the longer it will take to decide.

Start your presentation with, "Because you said you needed (a hot button), I recommend you get (the ideal solution). That's a power statement that leads to the consumer being confident in what you have offered to them.

Part 4 - Assuming the Close

In the movie "Glengarry Glen Ross" Alec Baldwin's character tells the rag-tag sales crew, "You got the prospects coming in. You think they came in to get out of the rain? A guy don't walk on the lot unless he wants to buy."

I agree. Although this is a crude scene that is very much over-dramatized, the point is made. Prospects have some level of interest in what it is you're selling; otherwise, they wouldn't have called, gone online, or shown up to start looking. You have their attention for at least one opportunity.

If you go into each sales call with the assumption that they are buyers, then your transaction will go a lot smoother. You also are putting out a vibe of them doing business with you and doing it today if at all possible. The lead will subconsciously pick up on that vibe, and act accordingly. On the other hand, if you go into a sale assuming they will still be shopping after your interaction, then the prospect will act as if this is just one stop of many. As long as you have positioned your offer to be the best (value, quality, price) for your potential buyer, then you have every right to act as if it's already theirs. How you vision that sale going is how the customer will take action. If you are focused on them having or wanting to think about it, then you're not assuming the close, and the customer will not buy at that time. I've seen it thousands of times over the years.

If you are the first place the prospect has stopped at to shop, save them the time of continuing to look around. Because if they buy from you, they can put the whole thing to bed. If the buyer has been somewhere else first, that's even better. You've seen the rest, now you got the best! Stop spending any more time on the matter, and let's get this done.

Part 5 - Closing Technique

Perhaps part of the problem with the average salesperson that has led the closing step to be such a mystery is that they don't know what to say to the prospect that would indicate it's time to sign on the dotted line. There are a large number

21 Simple Tips that will Take Your Sales to the Moon!

of salespeople that are waiting for the buyer to say, "I'll take it!" Although that could happen, don't expect it to happen very frequently. You need to ask for the sale.

But Brian, what do I say in order to ask for the sale?

You must be able to read the client and feel what type of closing question will work best for them. But be sure to use the proper question that fits the situation.

Is your client analytical?
Are they buying with emotion?
Does prestige or luxury become a factor?

Well, what would a great sales book be if it did not include some powerful closing techniques? This is a list of classic closes you can use to finish the deal:

Sales Close Techniques:

Assumptive Close:
This goes along with just assuming they are buying from the very beginning. Once the buyer has picked out a unit (or plan, or service), move right into the next step, assuming that they are moving forward.

Puppy-Dog Close:
This is where you use the return policy as a tool. Have them take it home or try it. "We do have a 30-day return policy. You can take it home to give it a try and bring it back for a refund or exchange." The reason it's called puppy-dog is that once they have the item in their possession, they aren't likely to bring it back. I mean, what kind of psycho would bring a dog back to the pet store?

Ben Franklin Close:
This is a close that has been mentioned many times in movies. The story goes that when faced with a big decision, Ben Franklin would list the pros and cons of the deal. If you are going to bring this out with a prospect, make sure you do it correctly. Here's how it's done: Frame it with, "Let's look at the pros and cons." Start with the positive. Remind them of all the parts of the deal that they like. Help them make this list as long as possible. Then switch over to the cons. DO NOT HELP THEM! This is their list to make. You will find that they will only come up with a few. Ideally, they won't get more than three to put down. But here's the secret: Whatever they wrote down is just the objection to overcome. If solved, you move forward! In most cases, the client will write down the money as a con. Fix that, and you can close the deal.

Credit Close:
Use someone else's money. In many retailers, there are additional savings by using the store credit card. Many buyers are likely to buy when there is a credit promotional instead of using cash or check.

Sharp Angle Close:
This is very effective after you have isolated an objective. The format here is to get a commitment. If you can overcome their objection, will that buy? It's very pointed, but if you have narrowed them down to a single obstacle, they have no other reason not to move forward. "If I can get your payment down to $500 per month, are you willing to take the car today?" If it's a "yes," get that done. If they don't commit, then you have another objection to find.

Switch Places Close:
Asking the prospect if your roles were reversed, what they do so the deal could be done. You'd be surprised as to what

they say. But whatever that answer is, it's the roadblock to overcome closing the sale.

Hurry Up Close:
This is associated with scarcity on the advertising side. Limited stocks, promotions endings, and seasonal events are all ways to get a prospect to hurry into action. But what most sales professionals don't realize is that uniqueness is also a reason to hurry. This is a perfect picture to paint if you sell used items or one-off pieces such as art or musical instruments.

Testimonial Close:
Getting current client testimonials is a great way to encourage the close with similar demographics. "Look what my other clients are saying about this."

Challenge Close:
Be careful here, but this can be effective with luxury items, or customers that are trying to keep up with the Joneses. The challenge is almost a miniature insult. You risk really upsetting someone, but if you have the right vibe, this can get someone to pull the trigger on a high-end item. "Maybe the S-Class isn't the right car for you. I have a good amount of stock on the C and E class units." Tread lightly.

Ultimatum Close:
Another risky close, but it can be effective as a last resort, or for prospects that have been leading you along for a while. "I believe this is the right plan for you. Are you ready to move forward?"

Take Away Close:
Using limited stock as the close, or even questioning if you can even deliver the item. "I'm going to have to check that we can even get this product for you."

Delivery or Install Close:
This is another close of assumption. Go right to the scheduling of delivery or installation of the product. This works well in retail stores that sell TV, audio, or do car electronics.

Any Questions Close:
Super simple to use. Right after your presentation. Give a slight pause, the length of a breath, and just simply ask, "Do you have any questions?" If they don't, start writing the order.

Power of Suggestion Close:
Tap into their imagination and paint a picture of them using your product or service.

Summary Close:
In this close, you repeat back to them the benefits that were important to them and tie it into your plan. "Because you said pregnancy is still a goal and that you travel across the country, I'd recommend the OneShare Complete plan that covers maternity, has an unlimited number of doctor visits, and has a nationwide PPO network under Aetna that will allow you to visit doctors around the country in that network."

Story Close:
Relate a story that has relevance to the prospect's situation. If you have had an instance where a hesitant client took action anyway, and they were overjoyed, that is the story to use.

You Know You Want It Close:
If you have a lot of rapport with your prospect, and they are in a good mood, you can pull this one out. It's very effective with men who are having fun through the sales process. "You know you want it, just go ahead and get it."

21 Simple Tips that will Take Your Sales to the Moon!

Trade-Off Close:
The classic "If I could… would you (buy)?" Simple close after you've been given an opportunity to overcome an objection.

Hot Button Close:
If you can dial into a feature and benefit that is incredibly valuable to your prospect, then highlight that as much as possible.

Just Suppose Close:
Another close from objections. The phrasing is, "Just suppose, we were able to (fix the objection), would you make the purchase?"

Qualifying Close:
This one is more of an early in the sales type of commitment. This can be used as a trial close near the beginning of the transaction.

The Reverse Close:
In this close, you use the objection itself to close. For example, in the case of a price objection, agreeing that a price is higher than competitors, which shows the quality of the piece.

Cash, Check, or Charge Close:
Assuming the sale, ask how they would like to pay. Very strong in retail, but it works in all industries. Even if you don't accept cash, it's likely that you offer finance or direct pay. Close on HOW they want to pay, not IF they are paying.

Alternate of Choice Close:
This is offering a choice to close the sale, rather than asking directly for the deal. The choice can be of two items: "So are we going with the black or the silver Benz?" Or possibly if

there was a three-tier option, like in insurance plans: "Would you want to go with the low, moderate, or high deductible?"

Reduce to the Ridiculous Close:
The more you divide a price by, the cheaper it sounds, and the more affordable it becomes. Speaking the price as a daily cost, sounds more reasonable than the monthly, or annual rate.

Secondary Question Close
Make the large decision smaller by asking a question that's less significant, but assumes the sale. "How soon were you wanting to have the TV delivered?"

Bargain Close:
It's not always wise to close on price, but if an item is on sale or there is limited opportunity, then creating an urgency based on a bargain is very effective. "This is a great (item) at this price. I'd hate to see you lose out on such a great bargain."

If You Say "Yes" Close:
Give them a reason to say yes that rewards having the item. "You can have the TV just in time for the Super Bowl, if we can get delivery set up today."

Yes-Yes-Yes Close:
Getting a series of agreements and "Yeses" throughout the sales process makes the large yes of the close much easier.

You Deserve It Close:
A very fun way to close the sale if you are dealing in a luxury item, or a special occasion. You have to have good rapport with the buyer, and say it in a fun way, "You deserve this!"

21 Simple Tips that will Take Your Sales to the Moon!

The Expert Opinion Close:
Sometimes citing an expert, trusted professional, or a celebrity as being a user of the item or service will put the client over the top. "Tiger Woods wears this same watch."

Accessory Close:
Make choosing an add-on the close because it assumes the close on the main item. This works well in the retail space. "Let's go pick out a strap for the new guitar. You like leather or cloth?"

Whichever close you use, after you ask the closing question SHUT UP! The one that speaks first loses. IT sounds funny, but it's an absolutely true thing. Ask your close very clearly, then wait for an answer. If you keep talking, then you're only back to selling more, and they will, "Have to think about it."

Takeaways:

- Closing is about reading the situation.
- The most powerful closing technique is to ask every time for the sale, at the appropriate time, and to keep quiet and wait for a response.
- Rehearse your closes so that you get comfortable using them, and to know when to apply different sales techniques to fit the prospect.

Sales Statistic: Close rates drop if the words "discount" or "contract" are used in a sales call.

Many sales agents don't realize the negative impact of certain words and phrases they use while selling. Mentions of the "discount" can only be a good thing, right? Sales closing statistics show that the close rates drop by 17% if the word is used in a call. For the word "contract," the decline is by 7%. Another phrase can have a negative effect if repeated 4 or more times is "we provide."

Exercise: Go back into the chapter and take the closing technique you feel most comfortable with, and write it to be your own for your product or service.

We have laid out a worksheet for outlining close to what you sell at <u>book.itaintrocketsurgery.net</u>

21 Simple Tips that will Take Your Sales to the Moon!

Chapter 20 - Walk the Talk: Practicing the Principles You Have Learned

"Whatever your mind can *conceive* and *believe*, it can *achieve*, as long as it rhymes."

21 Simple Tips that will Take Your Sales to the Moon!

"Life is about lessons and being able to positively apply those lessons to future decisions."

Floyd McLendon, Jr., Navy SEAL (retired), Professional Speaker, and bestselling coauthor of "Hard Earned Lessons"

Purpose: In this chapter, we will discuss the importance of implementing what you have learned.

How often have you run into a man or woman who's been successful with helping others by saying one thing and then doing something different? Oh, you haven't? That's probably because it's not a real thing!

What's more common is that the principles that are taught must also be acted upon; otherwise, without the right actions being put into practice, the materials will be dumped like a prom date. This is especially true if you're in a position of authority; it is of utmost importance to lead by example if you want to create a winning sales culture.

Walking the talk and practicing what you've learned will have these benefits:

Support of the Principles You've Learned Based on Results

As an example, if you just read a lesson on closing skills (I know a guy who writes sales articles and books), then you start using what you've read, then use those skills to close deals, you gain the trust of yourself and others in your abilities.

Fully Understanding the Principles

When we first are exposed to new information, whether it's by seeing, hearing, or reading, we get an idea about the concepts. But we must actually get the desire to act. Implementation is the way we cement the information in our mind. The process is referred to as: Head - Heart - Hands. Just gathering the principles isn't always enough.

Cohesion and Cooperation

This is mostly true in a sales team. When the group is all on the same page, the: departments, directives, and processes, run more smoothly. Even if you are not in a leadership position, you may have felt a better sense of comradery when both yourself and your colleagues are growing together.

Respect

When others can see that you are fully complying with the principles you have learned, you'll ultimately gain their respect. This is from clients or coworkers.

Disastrous Results of Not Practicing What You Preach

What happens when you learn new life principles and skills but don't take action? You're bound to run into one of all of these situations:

You may end up with a negative reputation as a lazy salesperson if you don't act on the ideas you're presented with. If you are a leader/teacher, you can come across as ineffective in the sight of your team if your actions don't match what you teach.

Those associates you expect performance from may very soon grow to resent you, especially a large investment or effort went into getting you the information. If you are a leader or manager, you face possible cases of rebellion that could grow since your team may feel they're being dictated to instead of led.

Or the next thing you know, there's money missing off the dresser, and your daughter is knocked up! I've seen it a hundred times...

How to Start Acting on Information and Principles

We are continually presented with massive amounts of content. When you hear something that resonates with you, the simplest part is to outline what you have learned and your expectations. Take a moment to decipher the principles you've been presented. That old saying, "Knowing is half the battle," is what we are talking about.

It may take a lot of effort to really walk the talk and practice the behaviors, so the next step is to find the inspiration. This comes from imaging the results you aspire to achieve. This should be very exciting!

Lastly comes the implementation. You can get started by creating a simple to execute plan with daily actions. Getting these small wins helps to build positive results on a daily basis with only a small effort.

More Tips for Action Items

Start practicing and taking action within your immediate circle of influence and close group. These are the people you tend to have close connections with due to morals and belief systems. They will give you feedback before you begin taking action in the business marketplace.

Tackle each principle one at a time. Don't try to drink from a firehose. Use the faucet or garden hose.

Work hard to make what we have learned become a daily habit as part of your everyday life.

Once you've established one principle, then you can move on to something else. It's important to be able to speak to the greater benefits you are experiencing from implementing that particular principle. There is fulfillment when you can show others just what the results of the actions, thoughts, and behaviors you have learned.

There is an old illustration of the way people truly have learned a skill: Head – Heart - Hands

The Head is to understand. We have gained the knowledge of what to do.
The Heart is the desire. We have become inspired in what to do.
The Hands is the ability to take action. We have the ability to apply the skill.

Do not be discouraged that you don't see an immediate result. True change comes gradually. There may be times that you'll fall below your own expectations, but that's okay. If you are inspired by a new idea, design your plan, and work on it daily. Slow growth is still growth. When you look back

21 Simple Tips that will Take Your Sales to the Moon!

in a year of hard work, you'll be more excited about what you've done.

Takeaways:

- **Acting on what we've learned is the most powerful part of growth.**
- **Integrity is the alignment between our words and our actions.**
- **As you learn new things, think about how the information will be integrated into the setup of understanding, desire, and action.**

Sales Statistic: 81% of companies say productivity would improve with better process, skills, or competency training*.

An investment in training, whether by your company or yourself, is worthless if there is no action taken on what was learned. There are countless books that can be purchased for ten or twenty dollars, that many people will credit as being life-changing. The reason people make the claim their life was changed by a book, is because they acted on what was presented. Otherwise, without making moves on what we study, the words are only as valuable as the paper their printed on.

Exercise: What areas of your personal and professional life have you not been implementing the lessons you have learned?

There is a personal accountability sheet available at: book.itaintrocketsurgery.net

*Statistic Source: https://spotio.com/blog/sales-statistics/

21 Simple Tips that will Take Your Sales to the Moon!

Chapter 21 – SCALING: Growing your business exponentially

"The *Executive's Special* is soup made with jalapeno peppers, chili powder, salsa, cayenne pepper, and red onions to help rekindle the fire in your belly."

21 Simple Tips that will Take Your Sales to the Moon!

"The business needs to have the right tools in their toolbox to operate a real business. And in this case, those tools are systems. Without the right systems, the business's value is diminished. So if some of the tools, or the whole toolbox is missing, you've got problems."

Jeff Dousharm, Owner/Partner at No Coast Business Advisors and bestselling coauthor of "Exit Lever"

Purpose: In this chapter, we will dive into ways to scale our sales organically or exponentially

Sales teams in all companies and industries have one goal in common:

Increase their sales!

This is also known as Scaling. But the key to scaling is not in adding more clients, although that should be a goal. Scaling is putting mechanisms in place that maximize effort or duplicating in a way that far exceeds the incoming force.

As a company starts to develop its goal to increase sales, there are many ways that this can be done, but all those ways fall into one of only three categories:

Three Ways to Increase Sales:

1: More Transactions - Attract more customers or Close at a higher rate
2: Sell More to the Customers - Increase your items per transaction or your average sale price
3: Increase Customer Buying Frequency - Repeat clients, or subscription services

Sadly, many sales professionals and/or their managers are not visualizing what scaling in their company should look like. Not all ways to scale may be applicable at the same time, or not all industries have a scalable product. That's all okay. You just need to find the first step that is the most effective and develop the strategy for action.

1. MORE TRANSACTIONS (CUSTOMERS)
The first increase that many companies think of in their effort of making more money is getting more customers through our doors, on the lot, on the phone, or wherever your sales happen. The majority of advertising campaigns focus on increasing the number of client interactions.

There are several things you can do:

Advertising
If you are NOT advertising, then start. Work with a marketing company you are comfortable with to develop a campaign targeting your ideal clients. Tweak as it goes so that you're keeping your cost per lead at a respectable level for your business.

Close Leads at a Higher Percentage
Also, factor in how many leads it takes to sell the client. That is called "Cost Acquisition." This is a calculation for how many leads per sale. Closing 5-10% better has a dramatic effect on how your number of transactions. The single

biggest impact on closing better is to make your ENTIRE sales process easier.

Implement Follow-Ups
Statistics have shown that proper follow-up can increase your customer conversion rates by as much as 50%! Following up with non-sold clients is a gigantic opportunity. Don't let potential customers ever forget about you. Keep lead in your ecosystem for-ev-er. This will keep the doors for future sales open.

Encourage Referrals
These are literally free leads but of the utmost quality. By asking satisfied customers to share your info with others takes nearly zero effort, but if a happy client sends over a friend or family member, the close rate of that referral is incredibly high. A client that was pleased with your service will tell three friends or family members about your business, even without being encouraged. Imagine what would happen if you started asking them for referrals, or even better rewarding their efforts, as long as your industry allows it.

2. SELL MORE TO THE CUSTOMERS
In the retail industry, we called that "increasing the basket." Look at your business, and ask yourself, "How can I get every customer we interact with to spend more money during the sale?" You or your company has already incurred the cost of getting them to the point of buying, so you might as well maximize the deal for the client benefit, as well as the company.

If you were to take an objective look at all the add-ons and up-sells in your product, they all benefit the client tremendously. Add-ons enhance the product, and the higher-grade product has a much better performance. Never feel guilty about attachments or showing the high-end offer. Quality outsells cheap any day of the week.

Sell more by: Increase your prices - Add high-end products or services - Upsell - Attach accessories or supplemental products.

3. INCREASE CUSTOMER BUYING FREQUENCY – REPEAT CLIENTS, or SUBSCRIPTION SERVICES
Sometimes we get so focused on finding new customers that we miss out on the gold mine in our own book of business. It's drastically easier to sell to those people who already know and trust you. Capitalize on the hard work you've already invested in winning over loyal customers.

Here are some growth ideas:

Offer Client Exclusive Specials
Customer appreciation offers help clients feel an exclusivity. These are almost a guaranteed way to get a client back to your office. It'll be a thank you offer, plus selling them more in the process.

Add New Products and Services
Find out what your clients want that you don't currently offer. By increasing the number of products you have available, you'll have more chances to get them back onto a sales call. Your clients will feel heard, know that you're looking out for them, and thank you with cash money.

Regular Communication of Your Services
In most cases, prospects begin shopping on one item that you offer. That is usually what brought them in, but in almost all cases, not all they may need or want. Clients will need to know your full scope of product and service offerings. You will need to continue to reposition yourself on a regular

basis. You must also let them know about upcoming specials, new releases, plan updates, and whatever else is a need-to-know event. Keep selling them on the benefits of the products or services you offer.

Scaling Opportunities:
There are many opportunities that can be capitalized on in order to scale your sales and business. By working through all channels, you will begin to see potential in growing your offering. Here is an exercise of questions you can use to review that will dial in growth position:

What is my maximum customer cap? #

The number of clients you can sustain

What is my per-client revenue? $

Average revenue per sale

How many more clients do I need? #

Sales needed to hit your goal or customer cap

How can I make more per client? #

Look for ways to increase your average transaction, such as selling a higher quality product, or adding more items to the ticket like accessories, warranties, or additional services.

What bolt-on service(s) can I add within my industry, or related to it?

Are there any opportunities to add lines to your business, or is there some type of natural cross-sell that would benefit your clientele base?

What is a need in my industry that I can fulfill?

What is a need your clients continually ask for, but is not being fulfilled? This could be tangible needs like a product or service, or it could be intangible like an enhancement to systems that make it easier or more convenient to do business with you.

How can I replicate that service and sell it 24/7?

You need to be able to have your offering available around the clock. If you cannot feasibly sell your product or service around the clock, then you need to have the information available, and be able to capture a lead 24/7.

Can I offer an affiliate or referral program? If so, how much would it pay?

Many times, we can increase revenue by having an affiliate program that allows others to market your product or service, and you take care of the fulfillment and delivery. This is very popular in the digital product and training industry.

Can I create an agent salesforce?

This is becoming an agency owner. If you are capped at how many clients you can reach, then train an agent salesforce to sell, and take a small commission override on their business. This is the basis for every corporation in history. And before you start thinking of multi-level marketing (MLM) and getting a bad taste in your mouth, every organization in history is set up like a pyramid. If you don't believe me, then go watch any documentary on bringing down the Mod, and you will see those cork boards with the family shown in pictures.

21 Simple Tips that will Take Your Sales to the Moon!

How much would I make on each agent's client? (this overrides the sales of your staff)

What would an override look like that is fair to your agents, and fair to the manager of the salesforce?

How many clients can they service?

Just like your own, what is the agent's client cap? Another important question is to know what the average agent performance will be? This will give you a better idea of how many staff members it will take to scale your revenue to the target.

Where do I find these agents?

Recruiting is different in today's job market. It's not just a matter of putting out a classified ad. You have to be found. And depending on if you are paying commission or salary, your job posting may be different. You may even consider hiring a recruiting firm, or even staffing a position within your organization.

Could I teach or coach this?

There is a growing trend amongst successful entrepreneurs to sell their expertise. It has never been easier to be a consultant, especially with the expansion of Zoom. Even if you don't have the time to be a personal mentor, you can set up digital courses and sell them long after their creation.

How much could I charge?

The answer to this question fully depends on the level of time and value you are bringing. A digital course routinely sells for a one-time buy of $97 on up, or someone may subscribe monthly. If you are actively coaching one-on-one, then you can charge a handsome monthly fee. Set Up a team of coaches, and you give them a fee to do the hands-on work and still collect money each month.

In all these pieces, we are looking for ways that will grow our money machine without just adding clients ourselves, although we should be getting close to our own client maximum. The idea of scaling is to grow our business without growing more work. Scaling is shifting the work, and making moves that have exponential growth.

Takeaways:

- Take a global look at increasing your sales in
- Look at ways to maximize every prospect interaction for the fullest value.
- Expanding into a team will build exponential growth.

Sales Statistic: HubSpot Research found 72% of companies with less than 50 new sales opportunities per month didn't achieve their revenue goals, compared to 15% with 51 to 100 new opportunities and just 4% for companies with 101 to 200 opportunities. Hitting your numbers is a result of applying scaling techniques in all stages of the sales process, from prospecting through follow-ups and getting referrals.

Exercise: Write out your paths and opportunities to scale

You can get copies of the scaling worksheet at: book.itaintrocketsurgery.net

Conclusion: Some final thoughts on this thing called sales

"I knew I was successful when I stopped worrying about money...and money started worrying about me!"

21 Simple Tips that will Take Your Sales to the Moon!

"Don't ever let people know when you're down, or when you're hurt. When you fight, you'll push through and won't make excuses. Keep your game face on! When you're committed, you will not waiver."

Burton Hughes, Senior Project manager at New View Roofing, Motivational Speaker, and bestselling author of "Align Your Empire"

I hope by now you've been able to pick up some additional information and skills that can be added to your sales arsenal. The chapter contents are intended to inspire you with simple and usable techniques that anyone can start using and will make a difference in their sales success.

As a sales manager, you commonly hear sales pros asking, "How can I sell more?" While there are numerous ways to close more deals, or get in front of more prospective customers, what these salespeople are really asking is, "What can I do NOW, to write more deals?"

Here are some useful actions you can take NOW to elevate your sales skills, and sell more TODAY:

Set goals:
Make your goals as short as one day, then start to lengthen into monthly, quarterly, annually, and even further out. The next step is to apply whatever effort it takes to reach that goal.

Roleplay and practice with another salesperson or your sales manager:
This is a VERY overlooked area. Most salespeople are embarrassed to do this with coworkers but have no problem fumbling through a live sale with a prospect, which is where

the true money is on the line. Think of it as batting practice. You need to commit your skills and scripts to memory through practice. Working with the sales team helps everyone get better. All the cool kids do it. And by cool, I mean closers.

Review and study sales books and materials:
There are many great sales professional's groups on Facebook. These are great ways to learn and bounce ideas off other pros in your market, or others. The largest one is, "Sales Talk with Sales Pros," that's administered by my mentor Ryan Stewman.

Know Your Inventory:
If you are in an industry with physical stock, such as retail or cars, know all your inventory on hand; especially what's aged, in low supply, or brand new. Report any problem units to your sales manager. In a non-physical stock industry, know what is new, as well as, the hottest seller, or most benefit-rich plans or services.

Be First:
When you are not in a sales or service call, make sure you are available to be the first one to answer the phone, or greet them. There is no reason to stand at the back of the lot or be slow on the phone trigger. The top salesperson at each firm is usually the one that talks to the most prospects. Simple math there.

See EVERY Lead as a Buyer:
Assuming they are at your store or on the phone to buy is one of the most powerful techniques in all of sales. As a kid, we heard the cliche, "Assume is making an ass out of U and me!" Those idiots that said that were probably not closers. That prospect contacted you because they felt a pain point, and your product or service will ease or eliminate that pain.

21 Simple Tips that will Take Your Sales to the Moon!

Proceed accordingly, knowing that they didn't just show up on your lot or at your office to get out of the rain.

Stick to the Basics:
Once you establish your sales process, stick with it, and keep it simple. Use simple language and keep it concise. Talk to prospects as you would talk to your family (minus the colorful language, but that's your call). You don't need a lot of moving parts to work your deals, and you don't need long-form emails and messages to get your point across.

Build Value:
Your sales presentation should be value-based. Features don't build value, they only cost money. The benefits of the features have advantages, and that builds value. Start by stating the benefits, describing the advantages, then naming the feature.

Keep Great Notes:
Use your CRM for what it's designed to do. Taking great notes on leads will lead to more sales in the future, and make it seem like you've got a super memory with your prospect. This also makes it easier to rewrite a deal on the next plan cycle.

Ask for Referrals:
Always ask your prospects to refer you to their friends and family. You have very likely just worked with a person you would wish to have more clients of the same like and kind. Chances are high that they associate with other like-minded people, and with similar incomes and professions. If you are in a field that asks for references during the application process, then those references are also referrals.

Pass Out Business Cards Everywhere:
Leave them all over town. Put them in the restaurant bill when you are leaving a tip. Leave them on the bar counter. Take the opportunity to leave them at a place that allows stacks of cards to be put out, or tacked on a board. Setup a digital business card to keep on the lock screen of your smartphone. And make sure your business card has a link to your internet bio page.

Setup Referral Partnerships - AKA "Bird-Dogs":
A bird-dog shows the hunter where the game is and flushes them out. In sales and business, a bird-dog is a referral partner that will send you leads. Set them up in as many industries as you can that will help send leads to your business. Unless otherwise restricted, compensate them as well. People love to have "a guy" for their needs. If you can be the trusted professional for your bird-dog, then they will send you every prospect that even whispers needing what you sell.

Look for ways to partner with your competition as well. I purposefully work with as many brokers as possible in an agency that sells a competing insurance plan. I do so because their plan is incredibly selective. I can work with the prospects that get declined. The lead is happy that I'm able to help them, so my close rate is high. Plus, the referring agent is happy because I took care of the referral, and they were still able to make some money.

Send Letters to Neighbors of Your Buyers:
What if when your neighbor came home with a new car, then a week later, you got a letter or card from the salesperson that sold it, showing you where you can get a look at one of your own? It is not a turn-on for everyone, but there are many people in America who are trying to keep up with the Joneses. I know if my neighbor pulled up with a new luxury

21 Simple Tips that will Take Your Sales to the Moon!

car, I would want to take a look and a ride. There is always peaked interest in getting a new toy when someone you know gets one.

Become a Beast on the Phone:
Practice like crazy on your phone skills. Even if you are in an industry that has a showroom like cars or retail, many customers call in ahead of time. Those are leads that can be very easily turned into appointments. When I was selling musical instruments, many customers would call ahead to make sure the product was in stock ahead of time. By catching that call, I was able to set the items aside, and get the commission on an easy pickup sale.

If your company records your calls, set a small bit of time each week to work with your sales manager on listening to recordings to dissect what went good and bad. Don't be afraid of criticism. I'd rather work through getting better at my craft than work through a tight budget or bankruptcy.

In case you haven't caught on by now, all the exercise materials and worksheets are available at: book.itaintrocketsurgery.net

Acknowledgments

First and foremost, I want to thank my wife, Natalie. You have been the one that keeps the family grounded. Otherwise, I might spend too much time with my head in the clouds and not looking at the path ahead of us. You are the planner and integrator to my visionary.

Mason is my ride or die buddy! You are the reason I work as hard as I do, and my reason to keep a child-like sense of humor. I want you to have so many more opportunities than I did, and I am going to pull all the stops to make the best life for you.

Helen was my first real responsibility in life and kept me from going off the deep end. Without that, I might have gone too far.

Thank you to my brothers, Joseph and James, for being by my side throughout a wild upbringing. We were our own little gang, but we kept each other laughing so much, we never seemed to worry about anything.

Thank you to my McKittrick and Casey families for the huge positive support! I've always been able to present projects and share ideas, knowing that I will get the feedback I need, delivered with love.

Thank you to my Nawrocki, Floyd, and Wise in-laws, who treat me like a son and brother. Y'all have been my advisors over the last decade-plus, and I know I can turn to any one of the group for working through a difficult situation.

Thank you, Ryan Stewman, and the phenomenal Apex network! It's a true mastermind of not just entrepreneurs who are executing at a high level but an amazing assembly of folks who are incredibly giving. Ryan, you have shown us how to rise out of the tough times and expand our vision of what is possible for our lives. #weareApex

Thank you, Kathryn, for helping me bring a vision to completion. You pulled out the best from me, and showed some incredible patience during the process.

Thank you, Jessica, for advising me through my projects. You have shown me how to apply the skills for success within your own personality.

Thank you to the Apex coaches for inspiring me to see what winning looks like.

Thank you to my old managers who gave me a shot and my new partners who allow me to keep building. I've learned a ton about sales, business, and myself because of the opportunity to work with you.

Steve Lamb taught me to sell the feeling.
Joe Ruzic taught me to treat the team like family and friends.
Jack Watkins taught me to value relationships.
Thomas Lattanzio taught me how to keep my peace and sanity in the moment.
Shane Stanforth taught me to focus on activities instead of results.
David Hilbrich encouraged me to speak and train.
Chad Hansen encouraged me to write trainings to better the crew.
Craig Brown put me in positions to grow.
Dave Renicor taught me the importance of metrics.
Brad Barrett encouraged me to manage in my style.
Rich Kerr taught me about managing the processes.
Dan Crossland taught me to look for talent in all your people.

21 Simple Tips that will Take Your Sales to the Moon!

Jeff Hiller taught me how to keep my delivery simple, and to take it all in stride.
Rick Wallis encouraged me to act on ideas.
Don Rodrigues taught me to pick my battles accordingly, and not die on every hill.
Grant Sheffield taught me to use the knowledge of those that went before me.
Bruce Drummond taught me how to maximize a team member's talent.
Tommy Roberts taught me that every deal matters.
Matt John taught me the importance of a foundation of operations.
David Teitelbaum taught me how to let a team member work as their own individual.
Steve Patterson taught me how to recognize executions and patterns. Awareness - Training - Validation.
Greymi Rosa taught me how to let leaders lead.
JP Melton taught the importance of dialing it all in.
David Reed taught me the importance of simplicity in the approach.
David Lance taught me the value in looking for opportunities to get more clients.
Chuck Taggart taught me the importance of maximizing what you're already good at.
John Patton taught me that scaling can only happen after you have solidified your process.
Justin Alverson taught me to be like a brother to those I do business with.
Jason Lafferty taught me to see opportunities all around me for new business.

Lastly, thank you to Drewbie, Kris, Marc, Mike, and Tomas, aka The Goon Squad! Our daily conversations push me to excel at a level beyond what I could imagine on my own. Our conversations make me either want to take on the world or fall out of my chair laughing. But every one of them leads me to be better than I was yesterday. #goonsquad

About the Author

Brian has been in the sales profession for over 20 years. He got started in retail at the age of nineteen at a music retail store. Prior to that, Brian had spent the last five years working labor and food service jobs, trading his time for money. The gears switched in sales, and Brian learned to earn by using activity and actions to produce sales results.

From 1999-2001, and 2003-2015 Brian was a top-performing salesman, sales manager, and store manager for major retailers such as Mars Music, Ultimate Electronics, Best Buy, Guitar Center, and Office Max. 2002 was spent in car sales at Don Davis Arlington. All of Brian's sales positions were commission based, where the goal was to perfect each stage of the sales process, and maximize all opportunities for deals.

Brian got his insurance license in 2005, and from then until 2015 he worked part-time in the senior market offering Medicare health plans, while still being a top performing retail store manager. At the end of 2015, Brian left retail to pursue health and life insurance sales full time. This was a fantastic match of opportunity and environment! In the first four years as a full-time insurance agent and sales manager, Brian wrote over $6 million in annual health insurance premium (with the average policy holder being $5,000 in premium). In 2017, Brian began building a sales team, and in 2018 and 2019, the team produced over $10 million in annual health insurance premium.

As of March 2020, Brian currently leads his own brokerage, Insurance of Texas, which services life, health, and senior insurance plans for all 50 states, plus Washington D.C. The agency also offers Property, Casualty and Commercial plans for Texas. Brian also has platforms for insurance leads, and insurance agent recruiting.

In June of 2020, Brian took over at the DFW franchise of Insurance Training Academy, offering insurance license exam preparation. In 2021, they expanded into insurance

21 Simple Tips that will Take Your Sales to the Moon!

continuing education, and sales skills courses for insurance professionals.

Connect with Brian at BrianMcKittrick.com to find out more about his companies, read his blog posts, listen to podcast appearances and episodes, and connect on social media.

CPSIA information can be obtained
at www.ICGtesting.com
Printed in the USA
LVHW021059140522
718768LV00005B/20